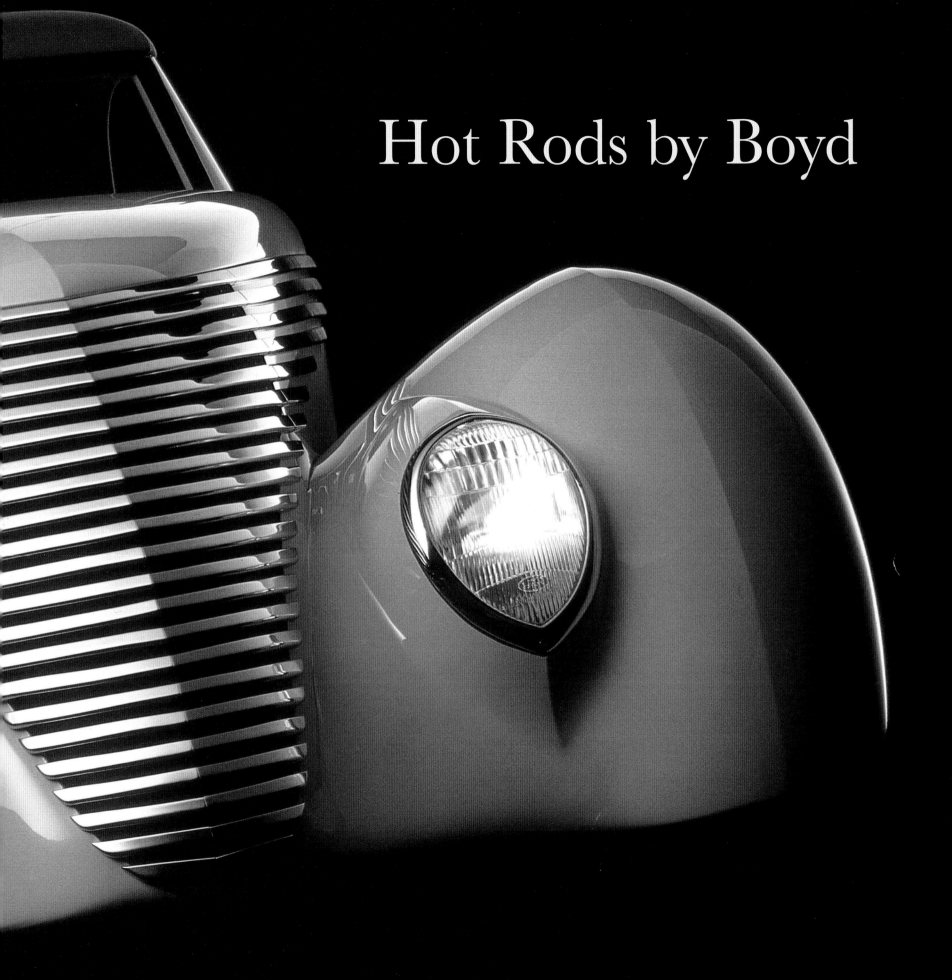

Hot Rods by Boyd

Edited by Tony Thacker

Designed by Kailay Yu

Printed in Hong Kong

Library of Congress Cataloging-in Publication Data Available

ISBN 09652005-6-6

On the front cover: Completed in time to show at the 1997 Oakland Roadster Show, the Boydster II was a full-fendered development of the 1996 AMBR winning Boydster. (Scott Killeen photo courtesy of Petersen Publishing).

On the frontispiece: Eric Geisert took this photograph of what were at the time vehicles in the Ron Craft collection. The photograph appeared on the cover of the May 1994 issue of *Street Rodder*.

On the title page: Probably one of the most beautiful street rods of all time, Fred Warren's Larry Erickson-designed DuPont Smoothster photographed here by Scott Williamson.

CONTENTS

INTRODUCTION

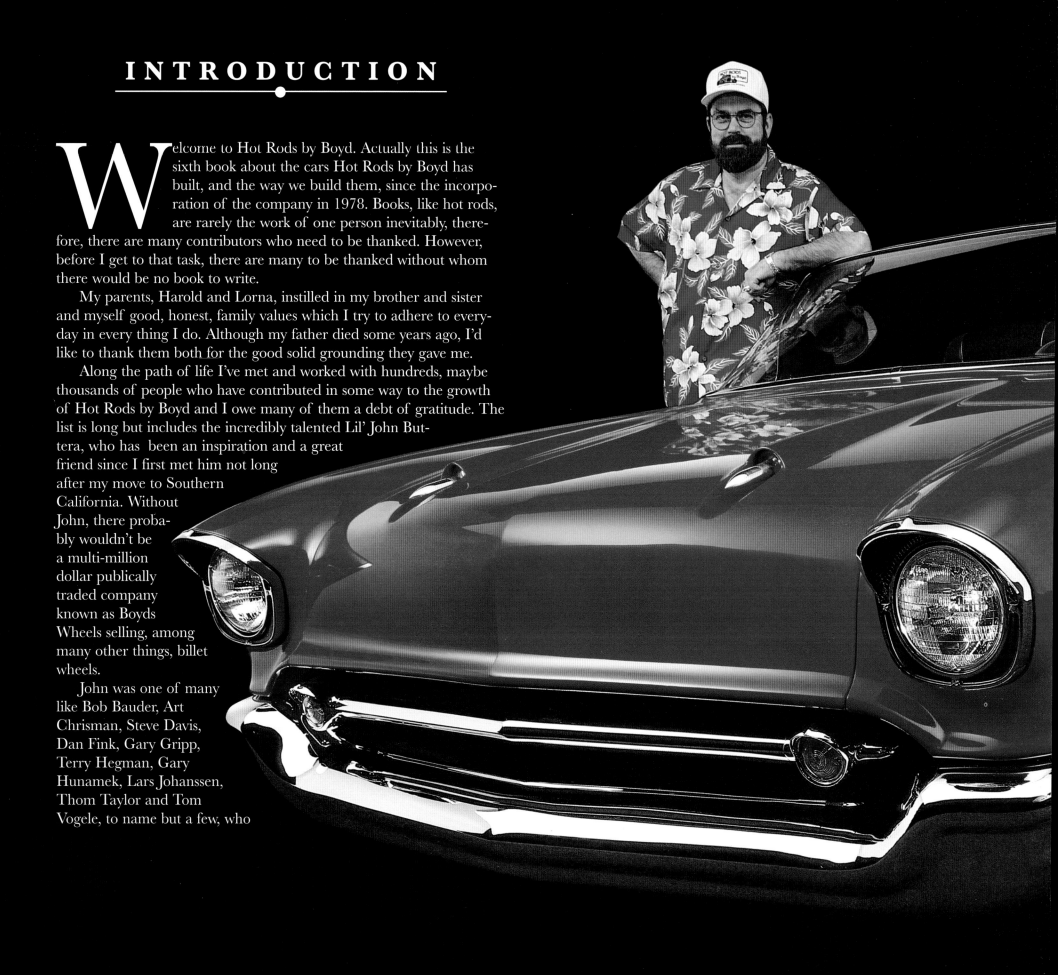

Welcome to Hot Rods by Boyd. Actually this is the sixth book about the cars Hot Rods by Boyd has built, and the way we build them, since the incorporation of the company in 1978. Books, like hot rods, are rarely the work of one person inevitably, therefore, there are many contributors who need to be thanked. However, before I get to that task, there are many to be thanked without whom there would be no book to write.

My parents, Harold and Lorna, instilled in my brother and sister and myself good, honest, family values which I try to adhere to everyday in every thing I do. Although my father died some years ago, I'd like to thank them both for the good solid grounding they gave me.

Along the path of life I've met and worked with hundreds, maybe thousands of people who have contributed in some way to the growth of Hot Rods by Boyd and I owe many of them a debt of gratitude. The list is long but includes the incredibly talented Lil' John Buttera, who has been an inspiration and a great friend since I first met him not long after my move to Southern California. Without John, there probably wouldn't be a multi-million dollar publically traded company known as Boyds Wheels selling, among many other things, billet wheels.

John was one of many like Bob Bauder, Art Chrisman, Steve Davis, Dan Fink, Gary Gripp, Terry Hegman, Gary Hunamek, Lars Johanssen, Thom Taylor and Tom Vogele, to name but a few, who

helped in the early days to establish a style which throughout the world has become defined as typical of Hot Rods by Boyd.

Besides all the people who have worked for Hot Rods by Boyd over the years, one cannot forget the customers. Indeed, the customers are the most important factor in the equation because without the customers there is nothing.

In the beginning, of course, there was candy man, Vern Luce, to whom I am indebted forever for affording me the opportunity to build our dream cars, finance them and be content to watch me drive them down the road as he rode alongside on his motorcycle. Vern was my first customer, and I'll never forget the opportunity he gave me.

Vern was followed by Jamie and Terry Musselman, Judi and Larry Murray, Don Smith, Nick Matranga, Bob Kolmos, Gary Newton, Dick Bauer, Gary Lorenzini, Ron Berry, Ed Burden, Bruce Corzine, Don Chiechi, Andy Chuha, Ron Craft, Dave and Dennis Aase, Larry Donelson, Billy Gibbons, Mike Guidry, Joe Hrudka, Butch Martino, Wes Rydell, Ara Sevacherian, Jim Sweeney, Dave Sydorick, Fred Warren, Buz Di Vosta, Michael Anthony and many others who have made my dream a reality. If I've missed anybody because of space limitations, please forgive me.

I also have a lot of journalists and photographers to thank who, with all the publicity they have showered over the years on Hot Rods by Boyd have been invaluable in growing the company. In particular, I'd like to thank Gray Baskerville for his unwavering support. Heck, we even chose a Baskerville font in his honor. Also, John Dianna, Harry Hibler, Tom Vogele and photographers Bo Bertilsson, Eric Geisert, David Fetherston, Rob Fortier, Scott Killeen, Randy Lorentzen, Tony Thacker, Steve West and Scott Williamson for their work that is included here. Also, I would like to thank both McMullen Argus and Petersen Publishing for access to their archives.

Finally, I'd like to thank everybody who currently works for Hot Rods by Boyd and the stupendous effort they put into every creation, meeting every deadline and building the finest hot rods in the world—Hot Rods by Boyd—we couldn't have done any of this without you all.

Boyd Coddington

FROM THE BACKYARD
TO WALL STREET

Born on August 28, 1944, Boyd Coddington spent the first few years of his life on a small, rented farm southwest of Rupert, Idaho, with his parents Harold and Lorna, his elder sister Klis and elder brother Wayne. According to his mother's journal, "This was a good farm and we did well."

It was a tough haul working the land back then but eventually Harold was able to purchase a nice 40-acre place. Lorna's journal reflects those years as, "Happy times." And in a way they were. There was that air of optimism that pervaded the fifties that made anything, even going to the moon, appear possible. Little did Boyd know though as he dragged home his first car where his interest in hot rods would lead him.

You could drive when you were 14 in Idaho in the fifties, but even before then, Boyd was itching to get behind the wheel of his own car. At the age of 13, without asking permission he traded his shotgun for a '31 Chevy pickup truck. Harold was so mad he made Boyd take the truck back and retrieve the shotgun. Eventually though, Boyd scraped together enough money to buy the truck back and started down his own personal yellow brick road.

While reading all the hot rod magazines he could get his hands on, Boyd learned quickly the art of horse trading and went through a string of cars. For example, the '40 Ford coupe, shown on the right, had a hot little flattie in it but he swapped in a '53 Studebaker V8 which was a

Right: One of Boyd's early hot rods was this '40 Ford coupe which came with a hot little flattie but he insisted on swapping it for a '53 Studebaker V8 which turned out to be much slower than the Ford it replaced.
Left: *Street Rodder* **called Boyd's Silver Bullet "The new breed of street roadster." Lil' John Buttera tweaked the Deuce rails to fit the contour of the '29 Roadster body.**

complete disaster because the flathead would run circles around the Studebaker. After seeing Norm Grabowski's "Kookie" T he took a Model A cowl and mated it to a Buick sedan and made a bucket out of it. Other cars he owned back then included a '46 Ford, a '53 Mercury, a '55 Chevy and a '55 Buick. They were simple times and cars were relatively cheap, but it was a mere prelude to what was to follow.

All too soon it was time to leave the comfort of the farm and take up a trade. After high school, Boyd took a body and fender class. However, next door was a machine shop. He kept looking over there and asking himself, "Why didn't I do that?" He went ahead and finished the body and fender class and worked in various local body shops, all the time thinking about becoming a machinist. Eventually, in 1964, he moved to Salt Lake City and went to work for May Machine and Foundry where they allowed him to serve a three-year apprenticeship. After which, having achieved his goal of becoming a machinist, his new goal was to move to Southern California where all those hot rods he read about in the magazines seemed to come from.

Boyd moved to California in 1967 and worked for Western Gear in Lynwood. At the time he was into off-road motorcycling, but soon after his marriage to Diane Ragone in May 1971, he brought home the basket case remains of a Model-T coupe. Life continued to be tough. Boyd and Diane had but one car between them, a '71 Pinto, and Diane would drop Boyd off at Western Gear before driving on to her job as a nurse in Maywood. The hot rods therefore had to be funded by money over and above their general expenses. In order to enjoy his hobby, Boyd did odd machining jobs and began working part-time doing fabrication for Larry and Roger Jongerius' J&J Chassis.

Eventually there was enough money to buy a house at 5935 Rexford

Avenue, Cypress, where there was a small garage in which Boyd could work on his projects. While working on his T, Boyd could often hear the sound of high-performance motors running. He didn't pay much attention until one day Art Chrisman walked into his garage. Art, who lived about a block over at 5935 Katherine, and was the man behind those motors, became a good friend to Boyd. Along with the move to the new house came a new job at nearby Disneyland.

The year was shaping up to be a memorable one for Boyd and to top it off, with the finished resto-rod style car painted silver and black, surrounded by a display of pumpkins and straw, he won the first of many trophies at the Long Beach car show in December.

The T coupe was quickly replaced by another box of wood—this time a 1915 center-door T sedan. Once again Boyd's attention to detail, coupled with the help of a few well chosen allies such as J&J which fabricated the chassis, Jim Babbs, who built the radiator and Jack Garrison, who stitched the interior, Boyd assembled a noteworthy rod good enough to appear in the August 1974 issue of *Street Rodder* magazine. April of that year had also seen the birth of a second son Chris, the first being Boyd Jr.

Ts and resto-style rods were what was happening back in the seventies and Boyd's next car of note was a '26 Tudor sedan. Photographed by Frank Oddo in front of the Magic Castle and the first car ever to be photographed inside Disneyland, it was also the first to feature a Boyd-built chassis. The car was also worthy of a three-page feature in the March 1976 issue of *Street Rodder*—there was no looking back now.

BACKYARD BUSINESS

Anybody who makes the move from a nice secure job, especially from a Utopian workplace such as Disneyland, to hang up their own shingle knows that gut-wrenching feeling of suddenly being completely alone. Besides, there were now four mouths to feed, son Gregory having been born in November 1977. Nevertheless, on the last day of October 1978, Boyd said goodbye to the Mickster and opened a new chapter.

With three magazine cars to his credit and one of them, the Silver Bullet, described in the April 1978 issue of *Street Rodder* as, "The new breed of street roadster," enthusiasts all over the world were asking, "Who is this Boyd Coddington?" If nothing else, the Silver Bullet was a true indicator of Boyd's ultimate direction. Described also as a striking blend of traditional styling, contemporary rodding and innovation, Silver Bullet, as I'm sure Boyd would be the first to agree, was heavily influenced by Lil' John Buttera's seminal white '29 Roadster.

Tony Assenza, in an article in *Car and Driver*, said of Lil' John:

"Buttera, among the first to build 'ultra' hot rods, is the spiritual inspiration behind Coddington's work. But Coddington has taken Buttera's approach and expanded on it by an order of magnitude. Both men are expert machinists. Both can turn the most mundane lever or dipstick into a work of art. Both have an eye for line and proportion that is reflected in cars of stunning beauty. Where they differ is attitude. Buttera is an artist—brilliant, occasionally erratic and often difficult to work with. Coddington is a scientist—methodical, unrelenting in the pursuit of perfection."

Boyd could also see the potential of what he was doing. Whereas Lil' John only really wanted to make one of anything and then move on to the next project, Boyd, right from the beginning, understood that the real money was in duplicating his work and selling it.

Boyd's number one with a bullet employed frame rails contoured to the '29 body by Lil' John, a cowl built up to accept a one-piece windshield, filled seams and smoothed fenderwells and numerous hand-crafted parts including a billet dash panel.

Left: Boyd's '26 T photographed at Disneyland by Frank Oddo, was described in the March 1976 issue of *Street Rodder* as, "A true masterpiece of the street rodder's art." Right: Known simply as "The Coupe," Vern Luce's '33 put Hot Rods by Boyd on the map when it won the Al Slonaker Award at the 1981 Oakland Roadster Show (Photo courtesy of Petersen Publishing). Inset: Boyd and the lollipop man who made it happen—Vern Luce (Photo courtesy of Tom Vogele).

The Silver Bullet also attracted the attention of a Southern California candy maker by the name of Vern Luce. "Vern was my first customer," Boyd says, "and I'll never forget the opportunity he gave me."

Vern grew up a So-Cal kid with gasoline in his veins. Despite a well-spent youth behind the wheels of numerous Model T Fords and even a '32 Ford roadster, he had to forsake his first love to learn the family business. Eventually, however, he got a handle on the lollipop trade and was in a position to indulge his passion.

Though Vern was usually to be found in casual clothes and work boots, often riding a motorcycle, his Newport Beach garage housed an impeccable and eclectic fleet of a dozen or so 1940s through 1960s classic American automobiles.

Boyd and Vern quickly became fast friends. In Vern, Boyd found the ideal customer: somebody with vision, enough lollipops to pay the piper and an attitude selfless enough to allow Boyd to build his dream car. Vern said of Boyd, "Somebody had to turn Coddington loose. There was too much talent there."

At the time, that dream car was nothing more than a series of Thom Taylor sketches (see Thom Taylor on Hot Rods by Boyd on page 38). However, when Vern saw those renderings, all he could say was, "Build me that car." Ultimately, those sketches, with input from Boyd and Lil' John, were massaged into The Vern Luce Coupe.

Other customers besides Vern came a knocking and Boyd knew it was time to move. What Boyd found at 6561 Orange Avenue, Anaheim, was almost perfect, a two-car garage with a single stall attached and room to grow. To begin with, there was just Boyd, however, he had managed to surround himself with some of the best talent in the business. Guys like Bob Bauder, Lil' John Buttera, Art Chrisman, Steve Davis, Dan Fink, Terry Hegman, Gary Gripp and Gary "Far Out"

Humanek who were on call to work their magic.

Before the coupe was even complete, everybody associated with its construction was of the opinion that a topless version, one that had a chance of winning the coveted America's Most Beautiful Roadster (AMBR) award, needed to be built. It just so happened that as the coupe neared completion, Boyd, like the card player that he is, had an ace or two up his sleeve. That ace in the hole was oil man Jamie Musselman and his wife Terry from San Antonio, Texas. Eventually, Jamie and Terry had Boyd build them more than a dozen cars. Said Jamie:

"I can go in the garage and drive cross-country in any one of them without a second thought. They may look like show cars, but they're real cars, quality-wise better than anything built in Europe or anywhere else. If I couldn't drive them, I wouldn't buy them."

In the winter of 1981, Boyd trucked the Vern Luce Coupe, a year in the making, 400 miles north for the annual Oakland Roadster Show. The response was staggering. Sure, people had seen nice street rods before—especially at Oakland—but they hardly compared with The Coupe. Boyd and Vern were rewarded with the Al Slonaker Award. Gray Baskerville, in *Hot Rod* magazine, said of the car, "It transcends the term hot rod. It's a three-dimensional work of 'heart.' It probably belongs in a museum and not jockeying for position on some freeway." As it happened, so that he could watch it go down the street, Vern preferred to ride his motorcycle alongside his car, rather than ride in it.

Boyd had certainly raised the bar in his chosen field and not by a notch or two: he'd raised it to Olympian heights. This was evidenced the following year when Jamie and Terry Musselman's '33 Roadster, known simply as "The Roadster," won Boyd his first AMBR trophy.

Not everybody was thrilled by the victory and some felt that the car, which set Jamie back some $85,000, had spoiled the business for the average, backyard rodder. Boyd had upped the ante to what some felt was an unacceptable level. As somebody said, "The game moved way uptown and few had the cab fare."

Boyd and Jamie were stung by such criticism. Both viewed themselves as rodders to the core, bona fide members of the fraternity. They were merely in a position to combine their talents to push the envelope

Left: Jamie Musselman, Boyd Coddington and Vern Luce pose with the "The Roadster" and "The Coupe," along with a handful of other important hot rods, for a photo shoot for the Aldan Shock Company (Photo courtesy of Tom Vogele). Above right: Jamie and Terry Musselman provided the wherewithal for Boyd to create his first "America's Most Beautiful Roadster" winner in 1982. "The Roadster" featured the metalwork of Steve Davis, Dan Fink and Terry Hegman. (Photo courtesy of Petersen Publishing).

further than it had ever been pushed before.

Time has proven that the shortsighted concerns of a few dissenters were unfounded. Certainly, Boyd had taken a quantum leap in attention to detail and style, but there have been many other subsequent winners of the AMBR trophy, which goes to prove that you can't censor art, it will happen whatever.

Similar in style to the Vern Luce Coupe but sans top, The Roadster, more than the Coupe, awakened the hot rod world to the potential of aluminum. Like a newly discovered mineral, aluminum became Boyd's preferred medium and from it, he and his team, which had grown to include Tom Vogele, now editor of *Street Rodder*, and Lars Johnasson, whittled everything that they could. What was left over Boyd sold for scrap—nothing was wasted. Even the wheels were handmade, milled on Boyd's Bridgeport from solid billets of aluminum and bolted to spun aluminum rims imported from Compomotive Wheels in England.

Prior to making his own centers, Boyd had used Center Line Champ-style wheels, but suddenly, here was a whole new canvas to paint on. And Boyd was a master at the mill—he hadn't worked all those years in machine shops without learning a trick or two. Orders for more of Boyd's wheels began to pour in and soon it was all Tom Vogele could do to keep up with orders. An empire was in the making but only Boyd could see the big picture.

They were already at work on a second car for Jamie Musselman, who said of Boyd,

"It's like coming across a guy like Rick Mears and buying him the ride equal to his talent. You'd hate to see a guy like that condemned to a life of third-rate rides."

Far different from The Roadster, the Musselman's chopped '32 three-window coupe had a traditional dropped I-beam axle and a nine-inch Ford rear. Nevertheless, subtle modifications were made to the frame, which was pie-cut at the cowl, and body which had its front fenders raised to accentuate the "rake" and was bobbed in the rear. Boyd himself whittled pedals, dash and other billet aluminum parts.

During the summer of 1982, Boyd was invited to take The Roadster to England. It also appeared on the cover of *Hot Rod* magazine, subtitled, "World's Largest Automotive Magazine." Needless to say, Boyd's reputation was rapidly reaching a far wider than audience than *Hot Rod*'s circulation of one million readers.

Customers became much more frequent now. To cope with the increased workload, Boyd built a chassis shop for Lars, a body shop for fellow Swede, Jarmo Pulkkinen, and closed in a lean-to where he had a small office. Eventually, a rented building on Electric Avenue housed the body and paint shop.

Early on, Boyd understood the importance of magazine recognition and the value of advertising through editorial. Hence, in 1983, Hot Rods by Boyd embarked upon the build-up of a yellow giveaway '32 roadster for *Street Rodder* magazine's Super Run. Again, subtle and

In 1982, Boyd was invited to take The Roadster to a show in England. Here, he watches it being loaded at Los Angeles.

unprecedented modifications were the order of the day. For example, the bottom two inches of the frame rails, along with the Deuce's signature reveal, were removed. The frame was also notched and pie-cut at the firewall so that the rails could run flat and be tucked neatly behind the grille. The body was likewise shaved and smoothed over.

The build-up articles ran throughout the summer of 1983 and helped to redefine the look of the hi-boy roadster. At the same time, Hot Rods by Boyd was also redefining the more traditional woody for motorcycle dealer Don Smith.

Restyled again by Thom Taylor, Don's '32 woody was almost a contradiction in terms in that the team chopped and smoothed out one of Henry's crate motors.

All the ensuing publicity from these cars was creating a name for Boyd and his fledgling hot rod shop. And the opportunity to make another run for the AMBR trophy presented itself when Larry and Judi Murray came knocking.

The Phaeton was in many ways Boyd's most ambitious project to date. Whereas the previous creations had all been massaged smooth, the Murray's Phaeton would encompass the creation of a completely phantom body—a two-door Phaeton—one which Henry Ford had never produced.

To create the body, Steve Davis and Dan Fink, who had subcontracted all previous tin work, married '33 roadster and Tudor sedan bodies into one of the most svelte Phaetons the hot rod world has ever seen. For this car, Tom Vogele carved the company's first set of billet aluminum front A-arms and uprights. It would be a rare hot rod by Boyd from now on that would utilize buggy-spring suspension.

All of the suspension components were anodized red to complement Jarmo's use of a new color in the paint lexicon, "Boyd Red."

Almost everything, from the Dan Drumm-covered aluminum top by Terry Hegman to the custom wiring by Bob Bauder was fabricated by hand. The workmanship and attention to detail were rewarded at the 1985 Oakland Roadster Show where Larry and Judi snagged the coveted nine-foot trophy.

The Murray's Phaeton was quickly followed by a similarly styled Deuce version for Bob Kolmos who, twelve years after it was built, is still driving his hot rod by Boyd.

OUT OF THE BACKYARD, ON TO WALL STREET

By 1985, barely six full years after hanging up his Mickey Mouse ears and going it alone, Boyd had a tiger by the tail and knew it was time to step up. The move was made to a 6,000-square-foot facility at 8372 Monroe Avenue, Stanton, California. Like the cars he built, the shop was attention to detail personified. The linoleum tiled floor was spotless, with areas for individual car assembly marked out in different colored tile, as was a huge, inlaid 30-foot-wide logo. A sign on the door read, "STOP! See Boyd First." And how could you not?

To begin with, just four people worked there, but soon the building was overcrowded with people and projects. There was also a steady flow of journalists and visitors from all over the world wanting to see for themselves this phenomenon called Hot Rods by Boyd.

The production of billet aluminum wheels had been gradually expanding, indeed, some of the machining was farmed out to subcontractors to keep up with demand. However, Boyd wanted to improve quality control and speed up delivery time. Later that same year, he installed four Takisawa CNC machines in a separate facility just a block from the hot rod shop at 8151 Electric Avenue, Stanton. Each costing $150,000, the mills were hooked up to a CAD/CAM system and the wholesale production of Boyds Wheels began. Pretty soon, a dozen people were working in the wheel shop.

According to Boyd, they originally made true knock-off racing-style wheels but that style wasn't for everybody and soon they made wheels with conventional bolt patterns. A set retailed for the unprecedented price of $1,695. Boyds Wheels were not for everybody but it seemed everybody wanted a set.

Pete Chapouris, a good friend of Boyd's also in the hot rod business, once said, "There's no money in it once you get past the brake lines." And, for most who have tried to make money in the high-profile but difficult business of building street rods, that is probably true. Somehow though, Boyd, with his gambler's intuition, strong memory and his automotive intelligence network makes it work. He's the consummate deal maker who always knows where to locate something and somebody who'll pay for it.

Tom Vogele on Hot Rods by Boyd

I was working for the phone company in Glendive, Montana, when I answered an ad in *Street Rodder* magazine for an associate editor. I drove out to California, worked two weeks for free and got the job. That was in 1980 and I worked there through the summer of 1981 when I left and went to Halibrand for a month before moving back to Montana.

Soon after my return, Jerry Dexter called to say that Boyd was looking for some help so I drove back out in an old '40 Ford farm truck into which I'd dropped a small-block Chevy. Despite my rough-looking truck, Boyd hired me. I was well versed in auto mechanics but I had no fabrication, machining or car building skills in the way that Boyd built cars. I guess it didn't matter back then because his own needs were not fully developed, so I did okay.

There were three or four of us there at the start: Gary Gripp who handled the engine building and Bob Bauder who came in to do wiring and run brake lines. When I arrived, Jamie Musselman's Roadster was in primer and my first job was to blow it apart for paint and chrome.

Our normal day was eight or nine hours, but when we were thrashing to get a car finished, as we did with The Roadster for the 1982 Oakland Roadster Show, we worked all hours until it was done. It was certainly the only place where I've worked where every day you had to flip a coin with the boss to see who bought lunch. I swear Boyd had a double-headed coin because it seems I was always paying.

Boyd has always been a hard worker though, and there wasn't anything he couldn't turn his hand too—machining or fabricating—he could do it all. Sometimes his decisions weren't always right though.

I remember we had taken Jamie's Roadster back to Atlantic City for the ISCA Grand Finale and we were on our way back in Riverside, California, almost home, when we stopped for gas. Well, the brake drums on the truck were white-hot, nevertheless, we tried to make it home. Needless to say, a few miles down the road I looked in the mirror and the truck was on fire. Besides The Roadster, the truck was full of car covers but without a thought Boyd just jumped right in there to get the car out. The truck burnt down and we had to drive The Roadster home.

Boyd was a good teacher also and he taught me how to weld and run the lathe and the mill. To begin with, I mostly made brackets, but when he took The Roadster to England, in 1982, he left me to build a frame jig which I then proceeded to use to build about a dozen frames. The fixture actually

Bob Bauder, left, and Tom Vogele with the chassis of the Super Run giveaway roadster. (Photo courtesy of Tom Vogele).

only held the frame rails, which we bought in, at ride height and located the front uprights, I had to fabricate everything between the frame and the upright. There was a ton of tubing which all had to be notched but I loved it. That was my whole life back then.

The basic design of the front end, I think, came from Lil' John Buttera but I'm pretty sure Boyd developed the rear suspension around a Corvette center section. We also had great communication. He'd only have to tell me something once and off I'd go and do it. When I was learning, I'd work things out in cardboard, get his opinion and get on with it. We were in tune with each other, it wasn't like starting from scratch.

The next major car I worked on was Larry Murray's '33 Phaeton. I made the first set of billet A-arms for that. Just carved them out of a solid hunk of one-inch billet aluminum on the band saw. Then I worked them by hand, as we did all the aluminum parts, rubbing them down with 600 grit before finishing them off with steel wool. Sometimes, I'd be doing that for days. What made jobs like that exciting though was the fact that we were actually creating stuff, doing things for the first time. Things we innovated looked simple but their appearance belied the amount of work involved.

The highlight of our day was the daily visit from Vern Luce. He'd come and sit on a stool in the corner and tell jokes or rant n' rave for an hour or two about politics. It didn't seem to matter whether you listened or not.

Eventually, the work increased to where Boyd rented a building on Electric Avenue in which Jarmo Pulkinnen handled the bodywork and paint. We also built another room on the back of the three-car garage where Lars Johansson began to build frames and modify chassis rails.

After Jamie's Roadster hit, we, of course, got into the wheel business and pretty soon we were assembling wheels from machined blanks of billet and rims imported from England. I think Nick Matranga's Deuce coupe had an early set. Of course, assembling cars was always a nerve-wracking experience because quite often they had never been completely assembled before they were painted. So a lot of work was done after the paint and you didn't dare drop a wrench—you had to think about every move.

I worked with Boyd for three years and there is not enough money in the world to pay for the education he gave me. The strongest memory I have of those times is of his energy and capabilities. It could have been a one-man shop—he could do it all—but his vision was much bigger than that. ■

Hot Rods by Boyd was cookin', and over the next couple of years the number of new customers grew steadily while established clients came back for more. For example, a '32 Vicky was built for Vern Luce, Judi Murray had a Deuce roadster built and both Jamie Musselman and Don Smith commissioned Boyd to hot rod them a pair of the rarest of all Fords, a B-400 and a C-400 respectively.

Ford made but 926 of the 1932 convertible sedan B-400s, which was a cross between a Phaeton and a Tudor. The bullet-riddled body for Jamie's car was purchased from Don Smith in 1986 and was eventually assembled into another beautiful Boyd Red creation. Unfortunately, however, the car was stolen and stripped.

When the remains were found, Boyd purchased them from Jamie and rebuilt the car, this time painting it black before selling it to Ron Craft, another long-time customer, from Texas. Eventually, the car was sold again to Michael Anthony of Van Halen.

Don Smith, meanwhile, had seen a Thom Taylor sketch of a smoothed over C-400 and, "Had to have it." In fact, Don's C-400 is actually a '33 Tudor sedan with a two-inch chop, reworked quarter panels and bustle—to give it that "C-400 look"—and the windshield posts and cowl from a '33 Cabriolet. According to Don, "Boyd could weld water," and the seamless, seemingly authentic creation which had more than 1,000 hours in the bodywork and paint, but less than $300 in chrome, was yet another jewel in Boyd's crown.

While back at the Orange Avenue shop a rather atypical car for Boyd to build was begun for Gary Newton of Newport Beach, California. Atypical because it was a full-fendered '27 T roadster with a tubular chassis and a big Ford V8.

For various reasons, progress on the car was slow. Late in 1987 the hammer went down as winter and the annual Oakland Roadster Show approached. Gary's a heavy-footed Ford fanatic and his Caribbean Blue T was stirred by a 427 SOHC motor.

Despite a great deal of effort and attention to detail, the car unfortunately did not take home the gold. It was, however, awarded Best in Class while Boyd was voted Builder of the Year.

Later that year, Boyds Wheels was incorporated as a separate business and the following year it moved into a 21,000-square-foot building. By now, Boyds Wheels was also machining parts for other companies. The products included Big Al mirrors and motorcycle parts for Boyd's equivalent in the two-wheeled arena, Arlen Ness.

Anyone who was hanging out at Boyds in those days could sense the momentum gathering. In the six years between 1982 and 1988, Hot Rods by Boyd produced a total of 16 cars. Along with diversification in the types of cars Boyds built, came an ever more diverse list of clients. The cars ranged from hot rods to a Cobra clone for Mark Barrett to concept cars for major auto manufacturers. They even repaired Ferraris for Ferrari North America which was located just a few miles from the shop.

In 1989, several more cars were completed including a pair of almost identical Deuce three-windows for brothers Dave and Dennis Aase and a roadster for Mike McEwen. But it would be a custom car which would take the world by storm.

Billy Gibbons, leader of a little ol' band from Texas, ZZ Top, had had his own hit in the early eighties with a '33 coupe called Eliminator which, along with an album of the same name and the award-winning videos, drove the band's worldwide success.

Now, with a design by Larry Erickson, there was a chance to do something equally important but wildly different. Based on a '48 Cadillac Sedanette, metal magician Craig Naff and the team at Boyd's hammered out a custom beyond comparison, one for which all of Webster's superlatives have long since been expended.

Unfortunately, for reasons unknown, CadZZilla was not exploited in ZZ Top's videos and did not enjoy the MTV exposure that Eliminator had. It has, however, been seen by millions after touring the world as the focal point of the ZZilla Tour, being featured in dozens of magazines around the world and featured in a special display at the Petersen Automotive Museum in Los Angeles.

Boyd's contributions to the hot rod industry, coupled no doubt with the creation of CadZZilla, were rewarded in the December 1989 issue of *Hot Rod* magazine when it named him Person of the Year.

Far from resting on his laurels, Boyd was just getting into his stride, saying, "I can't retire. What the hell would I do?"

Well, we know what he did. After driving CadZZilla cross-country to Canfield, Ohio, for the *Hot Rod* Super Nationals, he went on to win another AMBR trophy, this time for building Butch Martino's aluminum-bodied roadster. (see Butch Martino on Hot Rods by Boyd on page 19).

Butch, a resident of White Plains, New York, commissioned the car back in 1987. It did appear in bare aluminum at the 1988 Louisville NSRA Street Rod Nationals, but it wasn't until the end of 1989 that the fire to finish it was lit.

Working from a futuristic and consequently controversial Thom Taylor design, Crag Naff was once again the hand wielding the hammer, but this time the chosen medium was aluminum rather than steel—it would be Boyd's first all-aluminum bodied roadster. The sharply chiseled nose, which some pundits described as looking like a steam iron, divided the fors from the againsts. When it came time for the Oakland judges to bring in their verdict, they gave it two thumbs up awarding it not only the big one but also Best in Class (Radical Altered Roadster), Best in Show and Best Rod.

In 1991, Boyd was elected President of the Street Rod Equipment Association, a council of the Specialty Equipment Market Association (SEMA). To get his perspective on the state of the industry, *Street Rodder* reporter Rich Boyd was sent along to interview him. Rich's opening paragraph gives a clear insight into Boyd's world.

"A conversation with Boyd Coddington is full of frustration for those not patient enough to withstand frequent interruptions and constant distractions. His daily schedule, full of appointments, meetings and the constantly ringing telephone, is a whirlwind of demands on his time and energy."

Wheel production was up to 100,000 units, the machine shops were turning and churning out dozens of other related products, an apparel business was underway, licensing agreements were being signed with companies baring household names, Boyds first video was shot, a line of car care products—Boyds Ultra Violet—was introduced and seemingly dozens of other deals were being done—simultaneously.

The hot rod shop was equally busy. Another purple car, a '33 Vicky, was completed for Johnny Freund of Nashville, Tennessee, in time to

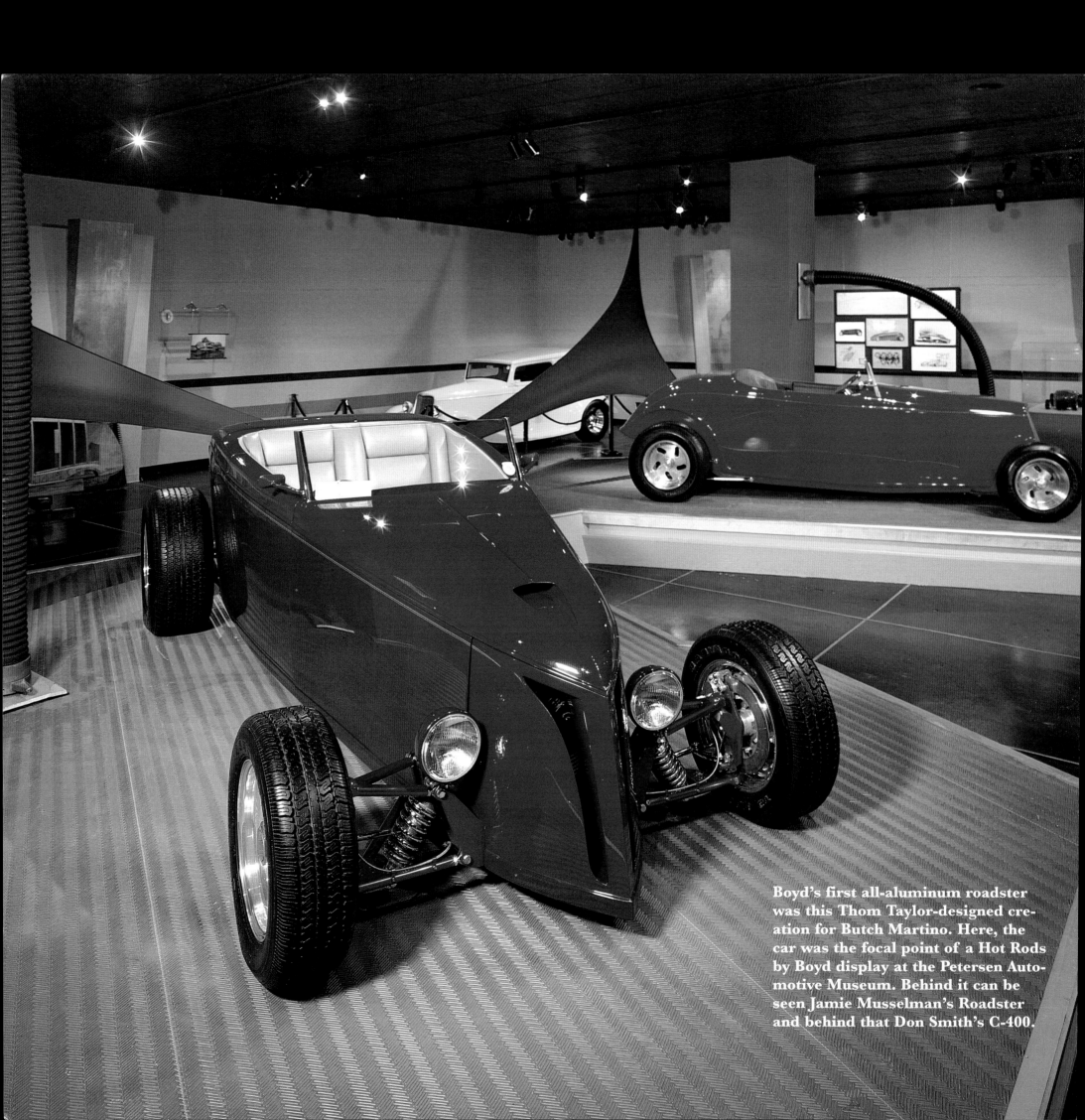

Boyd's first all-aluminum roadster was this Thom Taylor-designed creation for Butch Martino. Here, the car was the focal point of a Hot Rods by Boyd display at the Petersen Automotive Museum. Behind it can be seen Jamie Musselman's Roadster and behind that Don Smith's C-400.

Living back East, my introduction to Boyd was through reading about him in the various street rod magazines. I was so impressed with his work that I was telling all my friends that I wanted to meet this fella and someday have him build me a car. Mostly, everybody told me that was impossible.

I built and owned several cars back in White Plains, including a glass-bodied '32 Roadster. then a '33 three-window, a '32 three-window and then a '34 Victoria.

Eventually, perhaps inevitably, I met Boyd face-to-face in York, Pennsylvania, in 1986. Then, a year later, somebody reintroduced me to him at the Street Rods Nationals in Columbus, Ohio, and I asked him about the possibility of building an aluminum-bodied roadster.

I told Boyd that I wanted something akin to a '32 Roadster only more streamlined—something narrower and not so roundish. and something handmade in aluminum.

I'd never been to California and the car was seven months into construction before I even came out here. He kept asking me to come and I kept saying, 'No, just build the car for me.' You see, we just clicked from the beginning and there was a trust there and the working relationship developed into a friendship that we still enjoy to this day. That's why I keep coming back. In fact, I consider him my best friend. Besides, he has the best craftsmen in the world.

The car was finished in 1989 and displayed at the Oakland Roadster Show in January 1990 where it won America's Most Beautiful Roadster.

I like to drive my cars and back East the roadster was a challenge. So the next car was completely different. It was an all-steel, full-fendered, chopped n' bobbed '34 Ford three-window coupe. While the project was being worked on, I was trying to pick colors. Naturally, I wanted Boyd Red but at the time I said it will be just another red coupe and for about a year I debated what to do with it. Finally, I decided I wanted to flame it. We did and it became a big success appearing on the cover of the July 1993 issue of the *Smithsonian* maga-

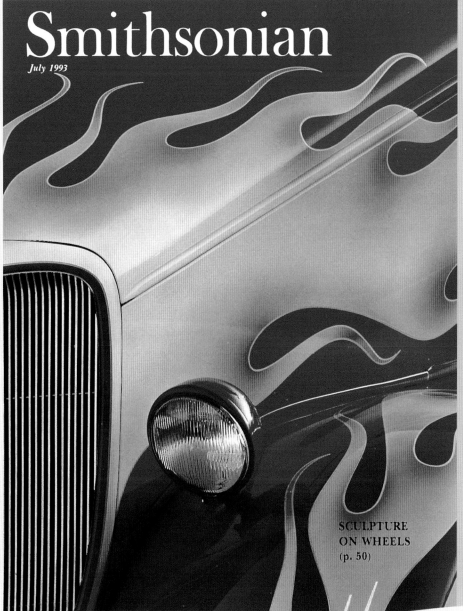

Smithsonian

July 1993

SCULPTURE
ON WHEELS
(p. 50)

zine. It think it was the only time they've ever run a car on the cover.

Currently, I own the '51 Ford Victoria featured on page 70 of this book. Again, I was interested in something different. Boyd was putting this together and when I saw it finished, I liked it and so we cut a deal. Right now we have a '40 Ford coupe on the go. We shaved the hinges, moved the wheels forward 2¹⁄₂ inches, and modified the hood, Basically, it will be another driver.

As for my future plans, I would like to do another roadster and go back to Oakland—try to win Oakland again. Of course, the hardest part of the whole deal is that Boyd keeps lifting the bar. It's worth the effort though, because being on the East Coast and hearing and reading about these people and then being able to build a car, take it to Oakland and win the America's Most Beautiful Roadster trophy has got to be the greatest thrill of this hobby. It's like winning the Super Bowl. ∎

Left: Butch's flamed '34 coupe on the cover of *Smithsonian*. Below: Butch's roadster in the raw, raw aluminum that is.

Porsche and Mercedes dismantlers David and Dennis Aase had Hot Rods by Boyd build them this pair of Deuce three-windows in 1989. Both had true "knock off" Boyds Wheels.

display at the 1991 Detroit Autorama. While Hot Rods by Boyd handled the chassis and extensive bodywork, the car went back to Tennessee to be completed. Also completed in 1992 was another woody, this time a '40 Ford for Dick Bauer. That car is featured on page 26. It was, however, a very different yellow car that was about to have an impact on the automotive world way beyond the street rod fraternity.

As you can read in Larry Erickson's comments on page 31, even before CadZZilla was complete, Boyd and Larry were already talking about another car. Another car which would cause the world, a world beyond hot rods, to became aware of the name Boyd Coddington. That car was the Aluma Coupe—featured on page 28.

Because at the time Larry Erickson was a designer in General Motors' Cadillac studio, it was hoped that Cadillac would supply a Northstar engine for what was shaping up to be Boyd's most controversial project to date. However, when Mitsubishi stepped up and donated a turbo Eclipse engine, many traditionalists cried foul and accused the builder's of sacrilege. A hot rod is as American as apple pie and not something to be powered by a foreign four-pot.

Once again, Boyd's vision proved to be beyond that of his detractors and the Aluma Coupe went on to be, without doubt, one of the seminal rods. After debuting in the Mitsubishi display at the 1992 New York Auto Show and appearing in literally hundreds of magazines, including many, like *Road & Track*, that would never normally feature a street rod, the Aluma Coupe opened doors into the world's major auto manufacturers. Without doubt it laid the foundation of public acceptability which has enabled Chrysler to build, in the Plymouth Prowler, a production street rod.

Soon, Hot Rods by Boyd, which had always employed the talent but

had never been seen as anything other than a glorified hot rod shop, was being approached by major auto manufacturers to play in their closely guarded, highly secretive world of concept cars. Propriety precludes us from revealing exactly which show cars Hot Rods by Boyd had a hand in building but you would be surprised by how many are household names. And to this day, Boyds Wheels continues to supply wheels to the automakers for use on their show cars.

Misinformed criticism notwithstanding, the Aluma Coupe did more to make the hobby of street rodding and street rodders, which had once been regarded as little better than outlaw motorcyclists, acceptable in the eyes of the public. As always, there were some head-in-the-sand dissenters but, Hot Rods by Boyd is a business and a business needs clients and if nothing else, the Aluma Coupe did two things: it drove the publicity, and it attracted clients. The pace at Hot Rods by Boyd began to turn frenetic.

On the road, behind the wheel of one of his creations, is where Boyd can be found most summers and in June 1992, he drove the Aluma Coupe back to Indianapolis for the Goodguys Hot Rod Happenin' at the National Hot Rod Association's Raceway Park. Many said the car wouldn't make it to Beach Boulevard—a couple of blocks from Boyd's shop—but make he did.

Also, 1992 saw the completion of the Cobra replica for Mark Barrett as well as a '46 Ford convertible for Buz Di Vosta who was in construction in Florida. The '46 is featured on page 40.

It was becoming a tradition to make an event of the "unveiling" of the latest Hot Rods by Boyd creation. In 1992 at the annual automotive aftermarket trade show held in Las Vegas by the Specialty Equipment Market Association, Boyd wowed the crowd with yet another home run.

Below: Bob Kolmos' '32 Tudor Phaeton was started at the house but finished at Monroe Aveneue. Twelve years later, Bob is still hammering it just as hard.

This time it was CheZoom. Another design from long-time collaborator Thom Taylor, CheZoom, as Thom explains on page 38, was quoted in *AutoWeek,* saying, "My thinking was this would be a contemporary version of the '57 Chevrolet. Even though it's from the past, it is a new experience, the fins, the chrome, the interior, the color; that's all new."

Despite their growing reputation for custom cars—Boyd saying in *Street Rodder* magazine, "We're going to have some fun cutting up those fifties cars"—the following year Hot Rods by Boyd turned out a string of hot rods including a '34 Chevy coupe for Mike Guidry and a rare-for-Boyd flamed '34 Ford coupe for Butch Martino.

Undoubtedly a real hot rod that any rodder would wish to grace his garage, Butch would be the first to admit that it was built to be a driver. Nevertheless, it was chosen by the editors to be the first car, hot rod or otherwise, to grace the cover of *Smithsonian* magazine. If Boyd and his small team of craftsmen had had a profile before, it was nothing to the recognition that the *Smithsonian* cover gave the company. Suddenly, they were written up in everything from *The Robb Report* to *USA Today.* Hot Rods by Boyd was even featured on a segment of Robin Leach's TV show, "Lifestyles of the Rich and Famous."

The car this time was Buz Di Vosta's "Roadstar," designed by Boyd's new chief designer, Chip Foose. Then a recent graduate of Art Center College of Design, Pasadena, California, Chip, the son of long-time famous hot rod and custom car builder Sam Foose, is the consummate car guy, wheeling, dealing, walking and talking cars—just ask his wife, Lynn.

Chip, who turned down several job offers to go and work for some of the major car manufacturers to work for Boyd designing and building hot rods, threw himself into the fray working all hours to continue and enhance the reputation of Hot Rods by Boyd.

His first effort was Buz' '37 Roadster featured on page 42. Like so many hot rods by Boyd, it too threw the critics into a tailspin. Here was yet another high-dollar, hand-crafted creation that some felt was beyond the capability of the average builder. But that's not the point. Not everybody can climb a mountain, but it's there to be climbed. Not everybody can build cars of the caliber of Hot Rods by Boyd, but we should be grateful that he has the ability to attract the talent and the customers to make the climb possible, inspiring us all in his journey.

As a full-time employee, Chip was in the enviable position of being able to devote the hours necessary to fully develop his designs and he worked diligently on the '37 shaping the body and interior bucks, grinding the headlight lenses and hand-detailing the gauges.

Just prior to the Roadstar's unveiling, Hot Rods by Boyd hosted a party at the Hard Rock Cafe in Newport Beach, California, to celebrate the creation of a billet aluminum guitar for Michael Anthony, bassist with the rock group, Van Halen. Somehow, while developing the Roadstar, designing wheels, T-shirts and dozens of other products for what

Gary Newton still owns and drives this 427 SOHC-engined '27 T Roadster. It was voted *Best in Class* at Oakland and was a *Sweepstakes* winner at the '88 Fresno Autorama.

was now known at the Coddington Companies, Chip found time to help craft two identical billet basses—one being given to the Hard Rock for display.

While 1993 saw the Coddington Companies move a block or two north to an impressive 100,000-square-foot complex of buildings centered around 8380 Cerritos Avenue, Stanton. It now comprises some 10 buildings covering 140,000 square feet. In comparison to the previous few years, 1994 was quiet on the car-building front. Hot Rods by Boyd completed a smooth yellow '33 Roadster for Dave Sydorick (featured on page 48) and continued to enjoy some unusual exposure.

For example, Aluma Coupe was featured in an episode of Tim Allen's hit TV show "Home Improvement." In that particular program, filmed at the Burbank Airport in Southern California, the Aluma Coupe, driven by mister "fixer-upper" Bob Villa, was pitted in a drag race against Tim's "Tool Time" '34 Roadster built during the show.

Also, 1994 saw a rather special exhibit at the Laguna Museum of Art in Laguna Beach, California. It was really the first such show which depicted the hot rod culture in a fine art environment. Jamie and Terry Musselman's '33 Roadster was chosen as representative of Boyd's contribution to popular culture.

After his work on CadZZilla, Craig Naff had moved from California back to his home in Woodstock, Virginia. There, he began work on another Larry Erickson design, this time a full-fendered '37 Ford. Unfortunately, the customer, Robbie Midollo, was unable to complete the project and it was transferred to Hot Rods by Boyd where, under Boyd's wing, Fred Warren stepped in to finance the completion.

Working together, Chip and Larry and the team at Boyd's massaged what became known as Fred Warren's DuPont Smoothster into what is generally regarded as one of the most beautiful street rods of all time. The effort was rewarded when the Smoothster was picked as Boyd's fifth winner of the America's Most Beautiful Roadster trophy in January 1996.

The completion of a number of other cars beside Fred's Smoothster took place in 1995. The list included Ed Burden's '53 Studebaker featured on page 66 and Butch Martino's '51 Ford Victoria featured on page 70.

The year was also a milestone in the history of the company. In September, reporting sales of $17.8 million, Boyds Wheels went public and began trading on the NASDAQ exchange. Meanwhile, Hot Rods by Boyd, at the time still owned by Boyd and his wife Diane, reported sales of $1.6 million. Boyd had certainly come a long way since starting his backyard business just 17 years prior. The name began to crop up regularly in the Business section of the *Los Angeles Times* as well as other financial journals like *Investors Business Daily*.

In a way of celebration, Cerritos Avenue was closed off to through traffic on September 28 and the first Boyds Extravaganza was hosted. The event, held to raise money for various children's charities, was a huge success and from that day forward would become an annual event.

Despite five Oakland wins under his belt, Boyd had yet to have his name on, rather than associated with, the winning car. All that was to change in 1996 when Boyd went back to the Bay Area with another Chip Foose-designed roadster, the Boydster.

Based loosely on some designs Chip had generated eight years earlier, the Boydster was Boyd's and Chip's attempt to reduce the Deuce to the bare essentials. In the May 1996 issue of *Hot Rod* magazine, Boyd was quoted as saying, " Buttera taught me to move my eyes from the front to the rear and back again when looking at a car. If nothing 'ugly' jumps out and grabs your attention, then you're on target." From front to rear, the Boydster evidences no "ugly" bumps; it's smooth to the extreme from its Lil' John-machined three-spoke wheels, to its hand-formed combination steel and aluminum body.

With a sixth Oakland win and your name at last on the nine-foot trophy, most people would go home content to kick back. Boyd is not most people. Before the Oakland Roadster Show was even over, he and Chip were about to embark on their most intensive program of car

Boyd has a way of attracting and building cars that make a difference, such as the Larry Erickson-designed CadZZilla for Billy Gibbons of ZZ Top. Craig Naff cut up a perfectly good '48 Cadillac Sedanette and ended up using very little of the original sheet metal to create what is unquestionably regarded as one of the all-time great custom cars. (Eric Geisert photo couresty of *Street Rodder*).

building since the company began. More than half a dozen complete, ground-up cars would emerge from the portals of Hot Rods by Boyd over the next twelve months—everyone of them a home run.

To begin with, the Boydster inspired a similarly styled '34 Roadster for long-time Texas customer, Ron Craft. It won the *Millwinder Award* at the Houston Autorama. Meanwhile, a fine '37 Cabriolet had been completed for Jim Sweeney. Then, in the summer of 1996, Boyd and Chip unveiled Sportstar, yet another creation that defies definition. Mark Vaughn of *AutoWeek* said, "Once again, Coddington has started a new direction for automotive design."

Sportstar, like the Boydster, was first transmitted to paper from Chip's fertile mind while studying at Art Center. The artwork was pinned to the wall of his studio where it drew many admiring comments. Eventually, the decision was made to build the car. Again, Chip whittled away on a buck which was subsequently shipped to Marcel DeLay where he and his sons wheeled and hammered the steel body. Featured on page 84, you could say that Sportstar is part Corvette, part Ferrari Testa Rossa, part Austin-Healey, but that would possibly be because your vocabulary is insufficient to find the words to adequately described what your eyes saw.

The hits just kept coming. Right after the debut of Sportstar, Hot Rods by Boyd completed a '41 Cadillac that went to Larry Murray and a '50 Packard woody for Larry Donelson. The end to a triumphant year came when Hot Rods by Boyd was acquired by Boyds Wheels Inc. At the time, Hot Rods by Boyd maintained a number of premier marketing and licensing agreements with blue-chip companies including

DuPont, Testors, Franklin Mint and Mattel. Mattel had, in fact, just launched the first four of a line of limited edition Hot Wheels featuring vehicles by Hot Rods by Boyd. The first four cars were The Vern Luce Coupe, CheZoom, Fred Warren's DuPont Smoothster and CadZZilla.

A banner year, 1996 was going to be hard to top, but the team at Hot Rods by Boyd are renowned for coming through. And sure enough, at that year's Oakland Roadster Show, Boyd showed, but did not enter into competition, the Boydster II. This screaming yellow full-fendered variation on the theme developed in the Boydster had many subtle differences from its predecessor. Featured on page 96, you can explore the design, the workmanship and the attention to detail that is both the hallmark of Hot Rods by Boyd and the standard by which all other hot rods are now judged—and it's a high standard.

Breakfast with Boyd is always interesting. His day starts early, usually around 5 a.m., but at 8 he can usually be found in the Restaurant Next to the White House. Don't bother him though because this is his time out. Besides, he's always playing liar's poker to see who pays for breakfast, and you'd better not disturb him. Breakfast is also a time for Boyd and Chip to get into a little "What if?"

"What if GM had been playing with the '59 Impala convertible's proportions two years earlier?" The resultant concept was "Boyd Air" a slammed, stretched and seductively lengthened marriage of '57 and '59 Chevy sheetmetal.

Dated photographs show a salvaged '59 Impala cowl sitting outside the hot rod shop in August 1996—Boyd Air was still but a concept. Then, in a conversation with John Dianna, Vice President, Executive

Publisher, Petersen Publishing, John said to Boyd, "We'll run it on the cover of *Hot Rod* but you've got to have it finished for photography by February 15." Never one to say no, Boyd said, "We can do it."

By January, just a scant four months from inception, Boyd Air, another completely hand-crafted car with barely a stock square-foot of sheet metal, was painted and undergoing final assembly.

Ever the showman, Boyd waited until April to unveil Boyd Air in a double-header celebration with an extremely subtle four-door '50 Chevy Hot Rods by Boyd had built for Wes Rydell. Also finished in the spring of 1997 was yet another giveaway Roadster, this time a bright orange '29 on '32 rails for *Hot Rod* magazine featured on page 106.

At the time of writing, Hot Rods by Boyd was busy working on a dozen or so projects including a '40 Ford convertible for Michael Anthony, a '40 Ford coupe for Butch Martino, an LT5-powered Deuce roadster for Dan Kruse, a '36 three-window coupe for Dave Sydorick, a '48 Ford convertible for Roger Ritzow and two cars for Fred Warren. One of the cars is a run-of-the-mill—if you can say that about a hot rod by Boyd—'34 three-window coupe. The other car, however, is yet another concept of Chip's which will no doubt create more controversy.

In fact, Fred's car is a front-engined roadster version of a design for a coupe Chip developed during his eighth term at Art Center. The final semester project was sponsored by Chrysler Corporation and Chip's concept and three-dimensional fifth-scale model, with hand-crafted billet aluminum wheels and suspension components and perfect paint, just blew everybody away.

Chip has already formed the wooden buck over which Marcel and his two sons have formed the steel body for Fred's roadster. Next, with a few minor tweaks, they will form the body for Chip's coupe which will be powered by a mid-mounted Chrysler Hemi.

With molten aluminum running through his veins, it was only natural that Boyd would eventually build an all-aluminum car. Designed to celebrate the Silver Bullet, "Silver Billet" will have an aluminum frame, aluminum '29 Roadster-style body and possibly an all-aluminum Corvette LS1 engine. With so many customer's projects taking precedence, the Silver Billet is not a priority. Nevertheless, as has been evidenced so many times in the past, the team of master craftsmen at Boyd's personal magic kingdom, Hot Rods by Boyd, have a way of making magic happen.

'40 FORD WOODY

According to designer Thom Taylor, "Boyd would just call up and say, 'Let's do such and such.' In this case it was a '40 Ford two-door woody, which of course Ford never made, it being one of my infamous what-if phantoms. Then he'd say, 'Just draw something up, oh, and draw some wheels while you're at it.'

"Of course, I didn't realize at the time that I was also helping to design his ever expanding line of wheels. Invariably, he'd direct me to, 'Do it in red.' Perhaps I asked if he wanted rubber or painted running boards, but usually there wasn't a great deal of communication before I would go to work on a side view. Literally, that's how it was.

"We were heavily into the smooth thing back in the very early 1990s when I designed this car for Dick Bauer, a Jaguar dealer from Anaheim, California. With the styling I was trying to smooth the Ford out, remove as much identification as possible and yet have it still be obvious that it was a '40 Ford."

Obvious it may be, this cherry lemon pie hides a host of details in its delicately fabricated wooden form which are anything but obvious. The biggest change, of course, came in the body which was converted from a four- to a two-door and in the course of construction chopped 2^1/$_2$ inches. Doug Carr at Wood 'N Carr handled the superb woodwork creating a truly distinctive vehicle.

Other, less obvious modifications include the glass treatment which, while more commonplace today, was a trend-setting move back then. If you look carefully, you can see where they V-butted the windshield glass and modified the side glass to resemble that of a hardtop. The rear of the body also came in for some unusual reworking in that the rear pan was rolled, or at least Doug formed such from wood to which were inset small rear lights. Notice also that the headlight rims were painted body color along with the grille and smooth running boards to give the fifty-something vehicle a contemporary, monochromatic look. A tan instead of the traditional black top emphasizes the updated design.

Because of the change from four to two doors, the interior, deftly handled in Boyd's own shop in brown and beige leather and cloth, sported a pair of Glide Engineering front seats which flip forward allowing access to the rear.

To begin with, the car rolled on a set of brushed aluminum wheels but as styles changed so were the wheels to be replaced with a polished set of Classic Series Boyds Wheels. Regardless of the wheel change and a change of owners, this a hot rod by Boyd anybody would pine for. ▬

Specifications

Original owner:	Dick Bauer	Body style:	Phantom two-door woody
Designer:	Thom Taylor	Manufacturer:	Wood 'N Carr
		Material:	Maple
Chassis:	'40 Ford	Modifications:	four-door to two-door conversion, $2^{1}/_{2}$-inch chop
Builder:	Hot Rods by Boyd		
Modifications:	IFS/IRS, tubular crossmembers	Top:	Beige canvas
		Front fenders:	Stock, bumper holes filled
Wheelbase:	112 inches		
		Rear fenders:	Stock
Front suspension:	IFS	Running boards:	Smooth
Shocks:	Carrera	Windshield:	V-butted, tinted
Brakes:	JFZ		
Rear suspension:	IRS	Front lights:	'40 Ford, painted rims
Shocks:	Carrera		
Brakes:	JFZ	Rear lights:	Inlaid in wood
Differential:	Corvette	Mirrors:	Boyds billet aluminum
Ratio:	3.08:1		
		Paint materials:	DuPont
Master cylinder:	Corvette	Painter:	Greg Morrell
Steering type:	Fiat rack-and-pinion	Striper:	Dennis Ricklefs
Column:	GM tilt modified by Boyds		
		Upholsterer:	Hot Rods by Boyd
Engine block:	'92 Corvette	Material:	Leather and cloth
Induction:	TPI	Color:	Beige
Headers:	S&S	Carpet material:	Mercedes cloth
Radiator:	Continental	Color:	Beige
Transmission:	Turbo 350	Seats:	Glide Engineering
		Steering wheel:	Boyds custom aluminum
Front wheels:	14 x 7		
Front tires:	Goodyear 195/70-14	Instrument panel:	Hot Rods by Boyd
Rear wheels:	Boyds 15 x 8	Instruments:	VDO
Rear tires:	Goodyear 235/70-15	Audio:	Sony AM/FM/CD

ALUMA COUPE

Described by J.P. Vettraino of *AutoWeek* as, "A Faberge Egg in billet aluminum," the controversial Aluma Coupe, while perhaps raising the hackles of many traditional hot rodders who would have rather seen it powered by a V8, certainly raised the world's awareness of hot rods and did more to promote the sport and Hot Rods by Boyd than any other vehicle ever built there.

Penned by Larry Erickson, the designer of CadZZilla, on a flight back to Detroit from Southern California, where he had been working on CadZZilla, the Aluma Coupe stretched the so-called envelope of hot rod design further than anyone had gone before and probably since. Like any great design, it stands the test of time looking as good at a recent Hot Rods by Boyd open house as it did at its debut on a turntable in the Mitsubishi display at the 1992 New York International Auto Show.

While the results were futuristic, Larry's original vision was a nostalgic combination of the Pierson Brother's '34 coupe and Art and Lloyd Chrisman's radically chopped '30 Model A. "The nose and grille," said Larry, "has that tipped-back look of the Pierson's '34, while the long hood and stubby back end is reminiscent of Chris-man's coupe. What's more, the coupe had a rear engine with the widest part of its body in front of the rear wheels which is perfect for a modern transverse engine and transaxle package."

Ironically, the intention had been to power the Aluma Coupe with an American V8. However, as the parameters of the car were being laid out, Harry Hibler, who was then publisher of *Hot Rod* magazine, introduced Boyd to Ron Kusumi who, at the time, was chief product planner in the United States for Mitsubishi Motor Sales of America. Ron, a California native and hot rodder at heart, had been harboring thoughts of a 3000GT-based show car when Hibler made

Above: The Aluma Coupe always looks cool and never more so than outside Mitsubishi's Cerritos, California, headquarters and just a few miles from Hot Rods by Boyd in Stanton, California.

Above left: The interior, featuring Mitsubishi Eclipse instruments, a Boyd steering wheel and Alpine sounds, was designed by Larry Erickson, shaped by Greg Morrell and upholstered in Connolly leather by Ron Mangus.

Left: The front end features in-board rocker-arm type suspension, an aluminum grille hand-formed by Pelle Forsberg and King Bee headlights.

the introductions. According to Ron, "Before that we were moving in a similar direction but on different tracks."

It wasn't long before Ron got the green light from Mitsubishi executive vice president Richard Recchia to support the building of the Aluma Coupe. Nevertheless, Ron knew he was walking a fine line between traditional hot rodders and within Mitsubishi itself, saying at the time, "It was a stretch for me to do this. I'm supposed to be head of product planning and people are wondering what I'm doing out there playing with hot rods. It was such a departure for a manufacturer's show car."

He needn't have worried: it was the right thing to do. The Aluma Coupe resulted in a great deal of positive publicity for Mitsubishi. Ron did, however, visit the shop once a week to watch his baby grow. Unlike most rods which are built around a pair of traditional frame rails, the Aluma Coupe's frame was constructed by Dave Willey from lightweight, round mild steel tubing eventually powdercoated medium gray as was the front suspension—quite untraditional.

Larry's original design proposed that the car would be a roadster. Ultimately, though, it was decided that a coupe would enjoy more integral strength and the shape was consequently developed from the two-tier style of a 1930's coupe into a single envelope. Interestingly, the design retains the hood break line evidenced in more traditional rods.

Larry Erickson and Larry Sergejeff subsequently combined their talents to build a wooden buck for the body which was shaped from .063-inch-thick 3003 H14 alloy sheetmetal by Marcel DeLay.

After a build time of only 11 months, the Aluma Coupe debuted in the Mitsubishi booth at the New York Auto Show to sensational

reviews. The world's media were all over the car and Mitsubishi basked in the limelight for supporting its construction. *AutoWeek* said Hot Rods by Boyd and Mitsubishi had joined forces to "Redefine the American hot rod." Little did anybody realize at the time that Chrysler Corporation would be the company to ride the trail blazed by Mitsubishi.

After New York, Hot Rods by Boyd had to get the car dialed in. The plan was for Gray "Your ol' dad" Baskerville of *Hot Rod* magazine and Boyd to drive cross-country from Stanton to the Goodguys Happenin' at the Indianapolis Motor Speedway. And that's when it got some bad publicity.

Outside Palm Springs, California, some Mitsubishi engineers were dialing in the motor when a rather over zealous police officer pulled them over and impounded the car. Not to worry, it was all a mistake. The car was retrieved the next morning and testing resumed in time for the ride cross-country which transpired with only one minor incident when a small oil leak caused a fire. The fire taught Boyd to always carry a fire extinguisher.

A couple of years later, Hot Rods by Boyd was invited to use the car in a season finale of Tim Allen's top-rated TV show "Home Improvement" which was a lot of fun. This particular episode called for Tim to drag race the Aluma Coupe against his just completed Magoo-built '34 roadster. The location was the Van Nuys airport just a few miles north of the Disney studios in Burbank where "Home Improvement" is filmed. Driving the Aluma Coupe was none other than real-life TV do-it-yourself star Bob Villa.

The Aluma Coupe has changed hands several times but occasionally it returns to Hot Rods by Boyd where it never ceases to amaze onlookers. The car, and indeed its design, always looks fresh and contemporary and remains a tribute to those involved in its creation.

Right: Designer Larry Erickson in the driver's seat alongside chassis fabricator Larry Sergejeff, try the bare aluminum coupe, sans roof (it was originally envisioned as a roadster), for size.
Above: Gray Baskerville seems always to be in the right place at the right time to record the construction of every major hot rod. Here, outside Boyd's Monroe Avenue shop, Gray captures the Aluma Coupe's tubular chassis fabricated by Dave Willey, prior to the fitment of the all-aluminum body.

Larry Erickson on Hot Rods by Boyd

I was born and raised in Cloverdale, California, where my father operated the Union 76 gas station and horse-traded automobiles. There was always excitement in his voice when he talked about them and there were enough around to instinctively know what was right and wrong. I'm sure that it was his love of cars that drove my enthusiasm.

I knew I could draw by the time I reached the sixth grade, but it wasn't until I got to high school that I realized I had some talent. Then I read an article about Art Center College of Design in *Car and Driver*. Until that time I didn't even know, if I thought about it at all, that there was such a career as an automotive designer, I guess I figured that design just happened.

Right away, I knew what I wanted to do, but as usual, I didn't do it right away. Instead, I misspent my youth racing, even did some Formula V. But somehow it didn't hold my interest between races, so eventually I enrolled at Art Center.

To help pay the tuition, I did some hot rod art. For example, a poster for the Bonneville Nationals. But I always felt my attempts were modest in comparison to Thom Taylor who I regarded as the "high priest" of the hot rod genre.

After graduation I received an offer from GM to work in their Detroit design center and so moved back to Michigan. With a regular income, I decided it was time to build a rod of my own. I planned to use an Experimetal steel '32 Chevy body and managed to talk Sonny Rinke into trading art for parts. Then, through one of those strange quirks of fate, Jack Chisenhall of Vintage Air saw my artwork and arranged a meeting between ourselves, Boyd and Billy Gibbons of ZZ Top to discuss CadZZilla. That was at the Louisville Street Rod Nationals in 1988.

The thing I remember most about that meeting, and the thing that I think elevates Boyd above the rest, is that when I was explaining to Billy how things in real life had to be different from the sketches Boyd said, "We can build anything you want."

Most people don't understand how much conviction it takes to say that and follow through. I still hold that image of Boyd's total conviction to building these cars.

Boyd and I worked well together on the construction of CadZZilla which was difficult with me being in Detroit and only able to fly to the West Coast occasionally. Consequently, most of the details were resolved over the fax. As the project neared its end, Boyd said he would like to build another car. What was intriguing for me was that sometimes people are interested in having you draw their ideas, others have no ideas and want only to build yours. However, with Boyd you work together and the result, as in the case of the Vern Luce Coupe, becomes, because of his commitment, something special.

The Aluma Coupe started out as just another hot rod but once I did the scale model it took on a significance—it started very strong and we got a good reaction. Often, when the conditions are difficult, things can go terribly wrong. I've had a few of those, but again, Boyd's commitment carried the project through, and as with CadZZilla the Aluma Coupe always stayed completely on track despite my long-distance involvement.

Working with Boyd I always felt there was a mutual respect and a shared objective and that's what kept the concept together. In the end the Aluma Coupe had an edge and a force which was as strong at the end of the project as it was at the beginning.

When it became apparent that this was going to be a significant car and would be in the Mitsubishi display at the New York Auto Show, I was disappointed that it didn't have a GM engine. Regardless of that, however, it was an extremely positive thing for Boyd and it gave him such a high profile that it didn't matter what engine it had and it showed, more importantly, what his shop was capable of doing. ∎

Specifications

Original owner:	Boyd Coddington	Transaxle:	1990 Mitsubishi Galant automatic four-speed with Boyd-built billet driveshafts and hub carriers	Rear wheels:	Boyds Tri-Fan 16x10	Color:	Lime-gold pearl acrylic lacquer
Designer:	Larry Erickson			Rear tires:	Goodyear P325/50R16	Painter:	Greg Morrell
Chassis type:	Mid-engine, tubular using 1³/₈-inch x .125 mild steel			Gas tank:	Custom	Upholsterer:	Ron Mangus
		Master cylinder:	Tilton	Body style:	Coupe	Material:	Connolly leather
Builder:	Dave Willey	Steering:	Fiat rack and pinion	Manufacturer:	Marcel DeLay/Hot Rods by Boyd	Color:	Tan
Front suspension:	Independent cantilever	Engine make:	1991 Mitsubishi Eclipse	Material:	.063-inch-thick 3003 H14 aluminum	Seats:	Hand-formed by Greg Morrell
Shocks:	Carrera coil-over	Type:	Twin-cam, four-valve	Grille:	Hand-formed aluminum by Pelle Forsberg	Steering wheel:	Boyds
Brakes:	JFZ twin-piston	Displacement:	120 cubic inches (2.0L)			Column:	1972-'74 GM van
		Induction:	Turbocharged	Windshield:	Scratch-proof aircraft-type	Instruments:	Mitsubishi Eclipse
Rear suspension:	Independent	Builder:	Russ Collins of R.C. Engineering	Rear window:	Plexiglass	Audio system:	Alpine Dimensions
Shocks:	Inboard Carrera coil-over	Horsepower:	320-330 horsepower @ 7,000 rpm	Front lights:	King Bee	Wheelbase:	114 inches
Brakes:	JFZ twin-piston	Torque:	275 @ 4,000 rpm	Rear light:	Custom	Track f/r:	58.3/61.5
				Mirrors:	Custom	Overall length:	157 inches
		Front wheels:	Boyds Tri-Fan 16x8			Overall height:	49 inches
		Front tires:	Goodyear P205/55R16	Paint materials:	House of Kolor	Maximum width:	75 inches
						Weight:	2,300 pounds

Below: Boyd behind the wheel on the highway somewhere between Los Angeles and Indianapolis on the way to the Goodguys Happenin'.
Right: A lot of controversy surrounded the choice of a turbocharged Mitsubishi four-banger but the whole essence of hot rodding has always been to find technologically sound ways to do things differently. The Eclipse engine was balanced and blueprinted by Russ Collins of R.C. Engineering.
Left: For a while, Boyd thought he had heated seats but 10 miles west of St. George, Utah, the Coupe was engulfed in smoke caused by a small oil leak. Now, Boyd always carries a fire extinguisher.

Joe Hrudka
CHEZOOM

CheZoom was conceived by Thom Taylor who said at the time, "I had just finished Frankenstude which is a somewhat similar car based on a '51 bullet-nosed Studebaker, so I was in that retro mode and drew this thing up. I pretended that I had been commissioned to restyle the '57 Chevy Bel Air hardtop and give it a contemporary look.

"I just did a side view and turned it in to Boyd knowing he had done CadZZila and had just finished the Aluma Coupe and was probably looking for something else to do. He looked at me," recalled Taylor, "and he said, 'You know who the perfect person for this would be? Joe Hrudka.'"

At the time, early 1992, Joe owned Mr. Gasket, one of the world's largest automotive aftermarket conglomerates. He also owned 20 or so classic Chevys and it seemed obvious that CheZoom would be a great addition to his collection. On a visit to Boyds Wheels, Boyd showed Joe Thom's rendering and that was all it took. Joe said, "I'll take it."

After locating and totally gutting a '57 Chevy, it was decided not to retain the frame. Instead, Dave Willey built a mild-steel rectangular tube chassis to accept Corvette suspension front and rear and an LT1 Corvette motor.

When it came to fabricating the body, likewise, very little of the stock '57 was usable, perhaps only 10 percent. According to Thom, "I wanted the front of the car to be as low as possible and embody the 'forward' look of the 1957-'59 Chryslers, which during that time had a great influence on GM styling. I also wanted to accentuate the rear fins because the originals were too subtle and, again, I liked the '57 Chrysler's better."

Master metal shaper Roy Schmidt created the new swoopy front fenders, with their wheels pushed forward, from 18-gauge steel and while the doors are located in the stock position, they were stretched 10 inches. The hood, on the other hand, retains the standard dimensions but was completely made anew without the classic Chevy's gunsights.

Above: CheZoom's powerplant was a "blue-painted" body color '92 Chevrolet LT1.

Left: Imposing from any angle, CheZoom takes the '57 fin to another dimension, evidenced by the 10-inch extension between the taillight and the bottom of the fin-tip trim. Numerous cuts were made by metal man Roy Schmidt in a pair of stock rear fenders to give the car that special "CheZoomie" look. Reworked '56 and '57 moldings were used in conjunction with hand-formed parts and inserts made by applying computer-generated chrome tape over silver paint. The top of the trunk was likewise extended 10 inches, as were the doors, to reduce the width of the rear cowl while the bottom was extended five inches.

Above: Initial mock-up stage shows that very little original '57 sheetmetal was retained.
Above right: PPG teal was a metallic/pearl version of the original '57 Chevy turquoise.
Below right: Dave Willey built this ladder-type frame around Corvette suspension.

To the rear of the hood is an electrically operated cowl panel which rises up to release the wipers.

A 1978 Chrysler Cordoba donated the windshield along with parts of the roof which were combined with parts from a '68 Plymouth Barracuda. The rear glass came from a Ford EXP hatchback and was mounted upside down.

As with any classic custom built in the 1950s, it was often the trim which made the car complete. To make CheZoom come alive, the team at Hot Rods by Boyd put in many hours to make the trim work. Original front headlight bezels were retained but painted body color. The lower bar is a lengthened and re-curved '56 Chevy item, whereas the top bar is '57 Chevy. However, to duplicate the filler panel, Boyd turned to Dennis Ricklefs who used a sign-making computer to cut grooves in a sheet of chrome appliqué. After painter Greg Morrell sprayed the fender section with silver, Ricklefs applied the chrome material over the silver base, after which Greg applied a clear coat to seal the trim which looks completely factory. The fender top trim is stock, as are the taillights, how-

ever, the section between the two was stretched 10 inches to compensate for the exaggerated fenders which were rotated to make them more dramatic. The rotation, and the position of the roof, caused the trunklid to fall short, so it, in turn, had to be extended 10 inches on the topside and five inches in the lower part. The rear pan was rolled and fitted with a sunken license plate.

Finally, the grille with floating bar, was formed in the time-honored fashion of rolling the body into two-inch tubing previously formed into the grille mouth. The floating bar was fashioned in the same way using tubing and two bullets—pure custom car. The background mesh was courtesy of Cadillac.

CheZoom debuted at a special party at the 1992 annual SEMA Show in Las Vegas.

Thom Taylor on Hot Rods by Boyd

I grew up in Whittier, California, very cognescent of what was happening in the car scene. In fact, for years I thought '53-'56 F-100 pickups came with Mercury taillights because every truck I saw had them. I don't know where the interest in cars came from but I know exactly when the hot rod thing hit me. It was the late-1960s and I happened to pick up a copy of *Rod and Custom* for reference and all of a sudden I thought a '34 Ford was the most beautiful thing I'd ever seen. I can't really explain that. Up to that point, old cars looked like Jeeps to me.

I didn't think I could draw real well but I loved doing it. I tried but I didn't think I was very good. What drew me to Art Center was my love of cars and I thought it would be cool to be at the beginning of the process of a car—to be able to see it before anybody else could.

The hot rod stuff happened because a mutual friend of Boyd's and mine, Bill Meads, who was a member of the Tourin' Tin hot rod club with me said, 'You should meet this guy Boyd Coddington.' At the time that I met him, Boyd was working on the Silver Bullet and I just started drawing stuff for him. That was probably 1976.

The first thing I think I drew was the billet dash for Vern Luce's '32 Vicky and then he and Lil' John Buttera milled it out. I did his logo while I was at school. I did two or three renderings and then I did some things for Lil' John. Through Boyd I got hooked up with Brizio and Pete and Jake. It just grew from there.

After a short stint with International Harvester, I decided to go free-lance and Boyd said, 'I'll guarantee you your first month or two's work and I'll set you up in the front of the upholstery shop.' He had a shop in Fullerton with Vic Kitchens and it said Hot Rods by Boyd right there on Orangethorpe.

It was impressive at the time that he had two shops, one where he built the cars and another where they did the upholstery. Anyway, I rented the front for a hundred bucks a month and that's what gave me the start to do this stuff full time. I was there until the end of 1981.

That was the time when the hot rod business was booming. Everybody needed a logo, they needed T-shirts and they needed ads. I've never to this day had to go looking for work.

What was so cool at the time was that Boyd was totally into it and we'd throw ideas back and forth and I'd go home and draw them up. That's how we did the Vern Luce Coupe. Boyd liked Jim Ewing's coupe and I suggested he build something along those lines but in doing so fix some of the things that bothered me about Jim's car. Things that I thought we could blend that would make it more contemporary.

I wanted it to have a chop like The California Kid but without the little knuckles where you have to bend the windshield posts. I wanted that to be straight like Jake's coupe but with angled posts, and that's what they were able to do. Originally, we were going to do a track nose but I think Lil' John talked Boyd out of that and so he asked me to draw it up with a '33 grille and that was incorporated into the design.

Out of that came Jamie's Roadster. Boyd had been preparing me for that saying, 'There's this guy and his wife from Texas coming over.' So they came over and they went in the back to look at Vern's Coupe, which hadn't been seen at that time, and I could tell right away that they were into the Coupe. And everybody had been telling us it was too bad that the Coupe was not a roadster because if it was, you could win Oakland. And I said to Boyd this is the perfect opportunity to build the Roadster.

I think the coupe had true knock-off Center Line wheels. I drew up some wheels and Boyd and Buttera made what I think were the first set of Boyds Wheels for Jamie's Roadster. And the rest, as they say, is history.

Years later, I was starting to push the bullet-nosed Studebaker thing and at the L.A. Roadster Show in 1990, I took my drawing of Frenkenstude to Boyd. I could tell he wasn't up for it and so I came up with CheZoom which I could see instantly he was into. Within moments he knew who we could build it for—Joe Hrudka.

A couple of things bothered me about the car. First, the wheels which for some reason I didn't get to design, and that belt line from the front edge of the fin forward to the headlights, which to me has too much arc in it. It's where everything comes together—the door to the fender, the A-pillar to the cowl, the cowl, the hinges for the doors—it all comes together right there. I think there was another way we could have worked it but it was too late by the time I saw it. At the time, the way the shop was configured, it was real hard to stand back and look at stuff. I never had the opportunity to really look at it until it was moved and by then it was too late.

In retrospect it's not supposed to be some Art Center styling exercise, it's a custom and I'm more comfortable with it now than I was when it was first built. Everybody involved with that car put in a great deal of effort and it's not fair to criticize their work. They did an incredible job. ■

Specifications

Original owner:	Joe Hrudka	Engine block:	1992 Chevrolet LT1	Grille:	Handmade from 2-inch tubing
Designer:	Thom Taylor	Induction:	Corvette fuel injection	Grille shell:	Hand formed
Chassis type:	1¹/₂-inch x ³/₄ and ¹/₂-inch .125-inch wall ladder	Horsepower:	300	Trunk:	5-inch section added to bottom
		Transmission:	700R4	Top:	Hand-formed using '78 Chrysler Cordoba windshield frame
Builder:	Dave Willey	Shifter:	Hurst		
		Front wheels:	Boyds Ninja 17x9	Front fenders:	Reformed using only headlight buckets and fender openings
Front suspension:	1985 Corvette	Front tires:	Goodyear Eagle SC P275/40R17		
Shocks:	Koni	Rear wheels:	Boyds Ninja 17x10	Rear fenders:	Rear quarters rotated upwards to raise fins
Brakes:	Corvette	Rear tires:	Goodyear Eagle SC P315/35R17		
Rear suspension:	1985 Corvette IRS			Doors:	Lengthened 10 inches
Shocks:	Koni	Gas tank:	Ford F-150	Trim:	Lengthened and curved '56 Chevy lower bar, '57 Chevy upper bar, center fluted area painted silver and lined with chrome tape.
Brakes:	Corvette				
Differential:	Corvette	Body style:	Two-door hardtop		
Ratio:	3.07:1	Manufacturer:	Hot Rods by Boyd		
Master cylinder:	Corvette	Material:	Steel		
Steering:	Corvette rack-and-pinion	Hood:	Custom fabricated without gunsights		
				Windshield:	1978 Chrysler Cordoba
Column:	Corvette tilt	Cowl:	Filled and flips up for windshield wiper access		

Rear window:	Upside-down glass from Ford EXP		
Lights:	Stock		
Mirrors:	Electrically operated		
Paint materials:	House of Kolor		
Painter:	Greg Morrell		
Upholsterer:	Jack Garrison		
Color/material:	Gray/leather and tweed carpet		
Color/material:	Gray/Wool		
Seats:	Modified Cerullo		
Steering wheel:	Boyds		
Instruments:	VDO		
Audio:	Kenwood		
Overall length:	201 inches		
Overall width:	72 inches		
Overall height:	48.5 inches		
Ground clearance:	4.5 inches		
Wheelbase:	115 inches		

Buz Di Vosta
'46 FORD

Outrageous rides are one thing but most hot rodders would agree that any self-respecting collection needs a little variety. There are certain days for driving cars like a roadstar, days when you can fully enjoy the thrill of putting the hammer down on a truly individual car. Occasionally, however, you need to be behind the wheel of something more sedate, something a little less flamboyant. It can still shout hot rod loud and clear and it can still have a lot more performance than most cars, but it is nevertheless discreet. Such is Buz Di Vosta's '46 Ford convertible which was completed in 1992 and was featured in the July 1993 issue of *Smithsonian* magazine.

Based on an original chassis fitted with Corvette independent suspension front and rear, Buz' fat porky six is powered by a 454 Chevy big-block crate motor painted red to match the exterior. With fuel fed by a four-barrel Holley carb, the motor runs through a Turbo-Hydro 350 transmission to a Corvette center section. The rack-and-pinion steering is likewise Corvette and the tilt column is another GM part.

Externally, Buz' quite ride is fairly stock except for some subtle modifications. For example, the headlights have been frenched, the hood has been shaved, as has the decklid, the running boards are blistered and custom rear lights have been frenched into the rear fenders. Also, the bumpers have been smoothed while the grille was painted body color. The chrome side trim is original, but all other chrome, with the exception of the smoothed out bumpers, has been removed.

Many hot rod convertibles have been fitted with a Carson-style top but Buz chose to keep his folding top original which seems to be a trend with some of today's rodders. Upholstered in beige material, the top matches the interior which is upholstered in tan leather. Interestingly, there is no stereo in the '46 but there is air conditioning which makes for comfortable cruising, especially when you're riding on a pair of Boyds Monterey three-spoke wheels.

In the shop for some minor repairs, Buz Di Vosta's '46 Ford convertible is, compared to some of his other cars, a nice, quite ride. Nevertheless, it is powered by a 454 Chevy motor and rides on a complete Corvette suspension system mounted to the original Ford chassis. The full-functional top is likewise original though recovered.

Buz Di Vosta
ROADSTAR

The year 1936 saw the last of the true roadsters from the stable of Henry Ford. The following year, while there were no roll-up windows, the windshield was fixed and the car became, in the eyes of purists, a hybrid, neither a real roadster, nor a cabriolet. Ford subsequently built only 1,800 of them worldwide and the few of those that remain are rare. Nevertheless, Chip Foose, who joined Hot Rods by Boyd as chief designer back in January 1993, had graduated two years earlier from Art Center College of Design, Pasadena, California, when he asked himself the perennial "what if" question, "What if a hot rodder were to apply his talents to a '37 Roadster then might Roadstar be the result?"

"I had worked with my father, Sam Foose, and Gene Winfield on a number or projects," said Chip, "including cars for the movies "Bladerunner" and "Robo Cop," but all I ever really wanted to do was build hot rods and customs. When Boyd offered me a full-time position—Roadstar was my first complete project to be built at Hot Rods by Boyd—what an opportunity."

Chip began by sculpting a $^1/_5$-scale clay model which he then used as a dimensional base to create a full-size rendering. The rendering and the model were then used as the datum for the construction of an unorthodox 116-inch wheelbase chassis fabricated by Dave Willey.

The frame, which was formed from both round and rectangular steel tubing, was designed to house a Cadillac Northstar V8 mounted in a mid-engine configuration and an equally unorthodox split I-beam front suspension.

Chip's concept for the suspension originated with those famous Miller Fords which looked better than they fared at Indy in 1935. However, the constraints of building hot rods to a budget dictated that the original design be modified in favor of split I-beams hogged out of huge billets of aluminum. Few people notice the indicators discreetly mounted in the I-beam uprights.

Chip, with the help of Bobby Bruhn, next constructed a wooden buck right on the chassis using plywood so that the laminates could double as both a measuring device and as a visual guide to the form of the body—the laminates predicted how the light would reflect in the finished paint. When the buck was complete it was shipped out to Marcel DeLay where they formed the body from .080-inch aluminum sheet.

Like all rods, there's a lot more under the skin than there appears and Roadstar is no exception. For example, both the hood and decklid, because of their placement, needed to cantilever away from the body in order to open properly. Consequently, Chip replicated the hinges from a '69 Camaro in billet aluminum. He even had to make the hood hinges 75-percent full-size because of space limitations. The grille was likewise machined out of 46 individual billet aluminum bars by Pelle Forsberg before Chip finished it by hand using a grinder and sanding block.

Even the headlights, which look like stock '37 units were, in fact, highly modified. Metalsmith Roy Schmidt made the steel buckets to match lenses which were subjected to eight hours of work on the glass

Left: Chassis fabricator Dave Willey is shown here working on the rear suspension assembly. Upper and lower control arms and hub carriers were all hewn from solid billets of aluminum. Around the rear-mounted Cadillac Northstar V8 is Chip's foam-board full-scale side view of the Roadstar. Below: Greg Morrell, squirter supreme, finished the cam covers, injector housing and floor pan in '85 VW Fawn Beige which contrasts beautifully with the custom-mixed candy tangerine from the House of Kolor on the chassis and body.

grinder by Chip who narrowed stock lenses one inch and shortened them 1 1/2 inches.

Not wishing to use an off-the-shelf windshield, Boyd turned to California Glass Bending which molded a windshield that has a light bronze tint as well as a barely visible peak in the center which washes out as it moves up the glass.

Finally, there was the interior which again was designed and hand-formed by Chip in foam before being covered in fiberglass. This buck was then turned over to Sam Trout who covered the swoopy seat package in Angus camel-colored leather. Something else that most people miss is that the seat splits horizontally and the upper portion, which is attached to the decklid, rises with the latter so as not to leave an unsightly gap when the engine compartment is open.

"We combined thirties flavor with nineties spice," said Chip describing the styling of Roadster to Gray Baskerville of *Rod and Custom* magazine back in 1994. And, looking back, Chip remains justifiably happy with his achievement, saying, "There are numerous innovations incorporated in Roadstar and it remains a piece of work of which I am extremely proud."

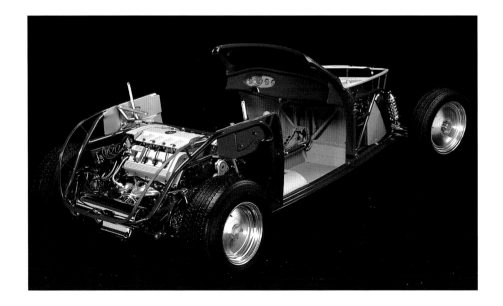

Chip Foose on Hot Rods by Boyd

My earliest recollections are from AMT in the sixties when my father was shop foreman for Gene Winfield over in Phoenix—I was three years old then. As a kid I remember growing up surrounded by the Ala Kart, the "Man From Uncle" car, the Reactor that was used on 'Bewitched" and the "Get Smart" Sunbeam Tiger was always at the house—I remember riding about in that car. We also had the Piranha rear-engined dragster. Those times definitely put hot rodding into my blood.

Actually, I was born in Santa Barbara, California, but we moved to Modesto when my father went to work for Gene. Then we moved to Phoenix, Arizona. Eventually, AMT moved their facility back to Canoga Park, California, after-which my father left them and we moved back to Santa Barbara where he worked for a company that built hovercrafts. After that he worked for Minicars, a company that built the first safety vehicles for the government in the late-sixties. At the same time he was building hot rods out of his garage at home—that's when he built that little '29 for *Rod and Custom*. I remember that car so well.

In 1970, he started Project Design and that's when I started to really hang around and work at the shop. I was seven years old then. That's when I met Alex Tremulus—the designer of the Tucker—and I fell in love with his artwork. Alex told me about Art Center and from that moment I knew what I wanted to do and that was go to Art Center.

For 15 years I was doing body and paint work with my father. I painted my first car when I was 12. That was a 356 Porsche, and I just kept going from there.

Eventually, I went to Art Center, but half way through, I left and started my own business called Foose Design in downtown Santa Barbara. I was doing illustration and design work. One of my clients, Stehrenberger and Clenet, asked me to go and work for them so I went there as a fabricator. Mark Stehrenberger was the chief designer there and Mark Neeper was his assistant. Well, when Neeper decided to leave he came to me and said, "You might want to talk to Mark about replacing me." I then worked as Mark Stehrenberger's assistant for three years—I learned a lot from Mark, particularly the rhythm of lines. I learned a lot from my father also, he's one of the most naturally talented designers I know.

I then went back to Art Center and it was very different from the first time. You're so intimidated and so overwhelmed—they pull the top of your head off and throw all this knowledge in—half of it is contradictory so you're confused and what you have to do is just start drawing and the more you draw the more you begin to understand how to separate the information. During that three-and-a-half years that I took off and went to work at what became ASHA Corporation, I learned how to shuffle that stuff—it was like a huge long internship. Going back to Art Center was then a whole ball of fun—I really enjoyed it because I wasn't struggling to learn how to draw; all you're doing is concentrating on design. It was a great time in my life and I made a lot of great friends that I know I will retain.

My eighth term industrial design automotive project was sponsored by Chrysler Corporation to design a niche market vehicle. They gave some examples but I chose to cater to a market that already existed—the street rod and muscle car market.

All this time I was aware of Boyd, but Larry Erickson introduced me to him at the SEMA Show. I graduated in December 1990 and then was invited to display my model at the following Oakland Roadster Show where Boyd reintroduced himself to me and asked me if I wanted to do some work for him. I worked for him on the side doing illustrations for magazines, wheels, all sorts of things. Boyd was giving me some neat projects and I was really enjoying working with him.

Meanwhile, ASHA, who had put me through Art Center, was changing to become more of an engineering firm rather than a styling firm and they didn't really know what to do with me. ASHA sent me to Ford where I sat on a sketch program. When I returned, ASHA wanted me to start my own business within their umbrella which I didn't want to do, so I accepted a job with Ford.

When I told Boyd I was leaving I had already designed the Roadstar and he said, "Let's talk." He put this whole project together and I thought, if I don't try it, there won't be a day goes by that I don't regret it." And boy it's been great. Every day is satisfying. Sure there are frustrating days, but I'm living my dream. The true satisfaction though is that with every vehicle that we build here we're also building a friendship with the owner and that's what's enjoyable. ■

Right: Sam Trout and Chip Foose combined their talents to form this exquisite camel-colored Angus leather interior. Parts like the shift lever bezel and horn button were hand-formed by Chip to match the center caps of the wheels. Even the Classic Instruments were hand-detailed. Chip also made the upper portion of the seat lift with the deck- lid to eliminate that ugly seat to body roll.
Far left: Sanitary engine compartment features a mid-mounted Cadillac Northstar V8.
Lower left: Keep looking and dozens of unusual little details keep appearing, for example, twin-I-beam suspension. (Photo courtesy of Randy Lorentzen.)

Specifications

Original owner:	Buz Di Vosta	Material:	.080-inch aluminum
Designer:	Chip Foose	Hood:	Aluminum
		Grille:	Billet aluminum
Chassis type:	Ladder with round and rectangular steel tube	Windshield:	California Glass Bending
Builder:	Dave Willey	Front lights:	Cut-down '37 Ford lenses in hand-formed buckets
Front suspension:	Split I-beams formed from 7075 aluminum	Rear lights:	Hand-formed
Shocks:	Carrera inboard cantilevered coil-over	Mirrors:	Located in windshield frame
Brakes:	Strange Engineering	Paint materials:	House of Kolor
		Painter:	Greg Morrell
Rear suspension:	Independent	Color:	White base with layers of candy tangerine and orange pearl
Shocks:	Carrera		
Brakes:	Strange Engineering	Upholsterer:	Sam Trout
		Material:	Angus leather
Master cylinder:	Corvette	Color:	Camel
		Carpet material:	Wool
Steering:	Rack-and-pinion	Color:	Camel
Column:	Boyds modified GM	Steering wheel:	One-off by Boyds with flush-mounted horn button to match wheel design
Engine/trans:	Cadillac Northstar		
Front wheels:	Boyds Roadstar17x7	Instruments:	Vintage Classic Instruments modified by Chip with candy tangerine over white faces and needles painted body color
Front tires:	Goodyear P245/40R17		
Rear wheels:	Boyds Roadstar 2 x11		
Rear tires:	Goodyear P335/35R20		
		Overall length:	145 inches
Gas tank:	Fabricated by Steve Davis	Overall height:	47 inches
		Overall width:	72 inches
		Weight:	2,700 pounds
Body style:	Roadster	Wheelbase:	116 inches
Manufacturer:	Marcel DeLay/Hot Rods by Boyd		

'33 ROADSTER

I t's not often that hot rods by Boyd, or those built by other companies for that matter, are subjected to the rigorous testing of the more mainstream automotive magazines. Nevertheless, hot rods by Boyd are built to drive and Boyd always welcomes the opportunity to test their mettle by driving them across country or putting them to the test.

So it was that *Motor Trend* called one day in the summer of 1996 requesting the loan of a rod to pit against a classic highboy roadster "rodstored" by Boyd's friend Pete Chapouris' company PC³g and the eagerly anticipated Plymouth Prowler.

Boyd elected to use Dave Sydorick's '33 Roadster as a typical example of his work and when Chip arrived with the rape seed yellow bolide, the contrast with the recently restored Doane Spencer/Neal East Deuce Roadster of Bruce Meyer, driven by Pete "P-Wood" Eastwood of PC³g, was staggering.

Dave's car, despite its loud color, is quietly understated in typical Stanton style with few extraneous hiccups beyond the rear-view mirrors and the headlights. Bruce's Roadster, on the other hand, is the face of actor Harry Dean Stanton, full of character acting lines and the lumps and bumps of years of use and some abuse.

To complete this trio of auto erotica, everybody was anticipating the arrival of the a Plymouth Prowler but the prototype puss in big rubber boots from Detroit was, unfortunately, still in Detroit. Consequently, it would be an old against bold test of different ends of the spectrum.

P-Wood was justifiably reluctant at having to pit low-tech against high-tech. The Deuce, after all, was originally built by Doane Spencer back in the early 1950s to compete in the infamous Carrera Panamericana Mexican road race. By installing Lincoln drum brakes, 16 x 7.5-inch wheels, and raising the engine, exhausts and gas tank to increase the ground clearance, Doane unwittingly spawned the classic "highboy" look that rodders continue to emulate more than 40 years on.

Left: In the summer of 1996 *Motor Trend* magazine invited Boyd and his long-time friend Pete Chapouris of PC³g to supply typical examples of the hot rods they respectively build for a back-to-back test against the then-new Plymouth Prowler. Boyd sent Chip along with Dave Sydorick's '33 Roadster while Bruce Meyer (left) brought his recently PC³g-restored Doane Spencer/Neal East Roadster. Considering the vast differences in age between the roadsters, not Bruce and Chip, both rods fared well against the Prowler with 0 to 60 mph times of five seconds for the hot rod by Boyd, 7.1 seconds for the Plymouth and 7.8 seconds for the flattie-powered Deuce. It's all a matter of different rides for different hides.

Left: Chip looks wistfully over the dash of Dave Sydorick's Boyd-built '33 Roadster as one of *Motor Trend*'s test drivers put the rod through its paces. The Roadster, which is powered by a Corvette LT1, managed an average of 63.9 mph through the 600-ft. slalom, besting the Prowler which only managed 62.5 mph. Lateral g on the 200-ft. skid pad was 0.87 for the Boyd-ster and 0.9 for the factory rod. According to *Motor Trend*, "The Boyd-engineered independent suspension is a delight to the eyes"—it obviously works as well as it looks. Above right: While auto manufacturers talk about moving the wheels of their cars out to the corners, street rodders have been doing it for years. In this case they're 16 x 7s on the front and 18 x 10s on the rear shod all round with Goodyear Eagle ZR tires.

Pete needn't have worried, the ol' 284-cubic-inch flattie, painstakingly rebuilt to produce 190 horsepower by Tommy Sparks, performed more than adequately, propelling the 2,250-lb. black bomber to 60 mph in 7.8 seconds and through the quarter mile in 16 seconds dead at 85.5 mph.

Despite its fibreglass skin, which is unusual in itself for a Boyd car—these days most have hand-formed steel bodies—Dave's car weighed in slightly heavier at 2,600-lbs. (incidentally, the Prowler weighs 2,864 lbs.), and with 300 horses of small-block Chevy trapped under its hand-formed aluminum hood, managed the sprint from zero to 60 in five flat and went through the traps at 100.5 mph in just 13.6 seconds.

Given the extremes of technology, the figures were not unexpected, nevertheless, the blackboy performed up to par. From here on, however, it wouldn't do so well because of the penalty paid for those long ago Mexican mods. With a high center of gravity, P-Wood would pay the price through the slalom, managing to top only 51.7 mph over 600 ft. Viewed head-on, it was a scary sight as straight axle suspension and the lack of antisway bars allowed for reckless body roll.

Needless to say, the '33 fared better because of technology. The front end is all Boyd-built, unequal-length control arms with Carrera coilovers and Goodyear Eagle ZR tires gripping like glue.

No doubt the Goodyears played an equal part in the success of the Boyd-built car on the skid pad, actually a giant concrete circle around which both cars drove at break-something speed. *Motor Trend* driver/tester Don Sherman managed to generate a lateral g figure of 0.87, which everybody was very pleased with.

P-Wood, however, had crossply tires to contend with. Also, the g forces caused the oil to blow out of the crankcase making everybody, including owner Bruce Meyer, think the engine was going to let go any minute. Thankfully, for P-Wood, and Bruce, it didn't and they managed a 0.67 figure which, given the Roadster's height and suspension, was a laudable effort.

Finally, there was a brake test, and as you would expect, yellow beat black, new beat old, power beat drums, and technology won out by 72

Specifications

Original owner:	Dave Sydorick	Shocks:	Carrera coil-overs	Front wheels:	Boyds Premier	Rear lights:	CPs
Designer:	Chip Foose	Brakes:	Wilwood		16 x 7	Mirrors:	Boyds
				Front tires:	205/45ZR16		
Chassis type:	'34 Ford	Differential:	Corvette		Goodyear Eagle	Paint materials:	DuPont
Builder:	Larry Sergejeff	Ratio:	3.08:1	Rear wheels:	Boyds Premier	Painter:	Greg Morrell
Modifications:	Lengthened and pie-cut				18 x 10		
		Master cylinder:	Corvette	Rear tires:	285/45ZR18	Upholsterer:	Boyds
					Goodyear Eagle	Material:	Leather
		Steering type:	Fiat rack-and-pinion			Color:	Tan
Front suspension:	Independent with unequal-length control arms			Gas tank capacity:	15 gallons	Carpet material:	Wool
		Column:	Modified GM tilt			Color:	Tan
		Wheel:	Boyds	Body style:	'33 Ford Roadster	Seats:	Recaro
Shocks:	Carrera coil-overs			Material:	Fiberglass	Material:	Leather
Brakes:	Power-assisted	Engine block:	Corvette LT1	Hood:	Aluminum	Color:	Tan
		Induction:	Fuel injected	Grille:	D.F. Metalworks	Instrument panel:	Boyds
		Driveshaft:	Custom	Grille shell:	Original	Instruments:	VDO
Rear suspension:	Multilink independent with anti-roll bar	Transmission:	three-speed auto	Windshield posts:	Boyds	Audio head unit:	Kenwood
		Shifter:	Gennie	Front lights:	King Bees	Speakers:	Orion

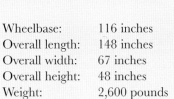

Wheelbase:	116 inches
Overall length:	148 inches
Overall width:	67 inches
Overall height:	48 inches
Weight:	2,600 pounds

Performance	
0-60 mph:	5.0 seconds
1/4 mile:	13.6 s./100.5 mph
60-0 mph:	128 feet
Slalom, 600 feet:	63.9 mph
Skidpad, 200 feet:	0.87 lateral g

feet. It took Sydorick's car just 127 feet to bring the car to a halt from 60 mph.

Dave's car was also two seconds faster to 60 mph than the Prowler tested by *Motor Trend* and two seconds quicker and 20 mph faster in the quarter mile. Also, it was faster through the slalom but a tad off on the skid pad, so Boyd was extremely pleased with the way Dave's car had performed.

But, there were no winners. It was not that kind of test. Each car was developed at a different time, using different technology for different purposes. Instead, each was a different expression of the great diversity that makes the street rod scene so diverse, so exciting and so much fun.

When it was time for Michael Anthony to slide behind the wheel of a real hot, and by that we mean one without fenders, he chose this black n' flamed '34 highboy roadster designed by Chip Foose. In his continuing effort to refine and indeed redefine the roadster genre, Chip developed some subtle styling changes which mostly go unobserved until they are pointed out.

For example, the steel chassis rails for Michael's roadster were carefully massaged by Larry Sergejeff to eliminate that notorious stock '34 "rock up," as Chip describes it, in the front, instead, there's merely a slight kick at the cowl.

Like most frames from Hot Rods by Boyd, the one under Michael's roadster sports fully independent suspension front and rear. In the back it's the usual Corvette center section, however, most unusual is the chili pepper milled into the billet aluminum cover. Needless to say, Michael is a fan of Mexican food. The third member is flanked by chrome tubular steel A-arms and Carerra coil-over shocks, a combination duplicated in the Mustang II-style front suspension.

Left: Michael's wife Sue suggested the hardtop and what a difference this aluminum piece wheeled up by Marcel DeLay makes to the visual impact of this flamin' hot chili pepper. Less obvious is the wheelbase stretch to 115 inches and the wedge-section applied to the body just above the lower beading. The wedge taper from zero at the rear to two inches at the cowl. The grille shell was also sectioned $2^1/_2$ inches and laid back "until it looked right." Michael was also specific about wheel sizes demanding 14s in front and 15s in back. Below: Traditional looking interior is jammed with audio equipment.

The chassis rolls on Boyds Vintage II wheels shod with 275/60R15 BFGoodrich Radial T/A tires in back and 185/60R14s in front.

Power for this flamin' hot chili pepper is provided by a 350 Chevrolet small-block which is fitted with a Holley carb, polished aluminum valve covers and a Boyds billet aluminum air filter assembly. Backing up the 300 horsepower motor is a 700/R4 automatic fitted with a floor-mounted Gennie Shifter.

Subsequent to the chassis being completed, the steel '34 Roadster body, a product of the Babbs Company, had its floor removed so that it could be dropped, or channeled, over the frame rails two inches at the front. A wedge section was then removed from the lower front portion of the body to allow it to sit parallel to the bottom of the frame. Of course, the lower front section of the cowl, including the bead, had to be reformed.

The chassis and body were then delivered to Marcel DeLay where a new three-piece aluminum hood was fabricated around a '34 grille which had been sectioned $2^1/_2$ inches and laid back until it looked right—about $2^1/_2$ inches. The grille insert, which hides a black painted radiator from Continental Radiator, is a fully polished stainless steel item from D.F. Metalworks.

Michael Anthony on Hot Rods by Boyd

I've always loved hot rods, particularly hi-boys, but being a musician kept me out of it until 1987 when I was working with the guys at BellTech to build an extended-cab short bed Dually-style pickup. That's when I met Boyd. We used his wheels on the truck and I didn't even know that he built hot rods, I only knew him as a manufacturer of wheels.

He invited me down to the shop and I was just amazed at the quality of the workmanship. So I'd go down there and hang out and before you know it, I'm thinking about a hot rod.

I bought a '34 Tudor but I didn't go to Boyd's, I took it somewhere else and it was a nightmare and took forever. That's when I decided to go to Boyd—he's top dollar but the quality is top notch, and he delivers.

When we agreed to build the Roadster I was able to have a lot of input. Chip's a great innovative designer but I wanted something traditional, or at least a combination of old-tech and new-tech styling, which is always hard to pull off. Both he and Boyd welcomed my input. For example, they wanted to mold the windshield posts but I thought they'd look better if they were attached in the traditional way. Also, when my wife Sue jumped in the car she said it needed a top. That's when Chip came up with the removable hardtop which is just great for keeping the sun off your head on those really hot days in L.A.

The car even has a carbureted motor which I wanted and Dennis Ricklefs flames. I've always wanted a hot rod with flames and they turned out perfect. The car still has many high-tech touches, though, like the drop-down rear license plate and Boyd's independent suspension which makes for a comfortable ride. In fact, it's a nice reliable ride and I love it.

Compared to the Tudor, building the Roadster was a total pleasure and it escalated my interest to where I purchased a '37 convertible so that I could haul my two daughters around. We had intended putting a rumble seat in the '34 but that didn't work out so I bought the '37. Unfortunately, the top proved too much trouble—it needed all the family to lift it on and off and when it was on we needed it off and when it was off we wanted it on—it wasn't the answer.

That's when I bought the B-400 that Boyd originally built for Jamie Musselman. That, of course, got stolen and stripped before Boyd bought it back, rebuilt it in black and sold it to Ron Craft. I still have that car, but again, it didn't quite fit the needs of our family because while there was room for four, there was no space for our stuff.

It was at that point that Dick Brogden showed me the '40 Ford convertible. It was flawless and seemed to offer the best of both worlds—convertible room for four and ample trunk space.

Once again, I've been fortunate enough to be able to work with Boyd and Chip to design a car that makes everybody happy. However, unlike the roadster, this one will be fully loaded with power everything, power top, power windows, heating, air conditioning—the whole works. And for power, Dick managed to find an alloy head motor from a Corvette Grand Sport. That should give it plenty of pep.

As for Boyd, he's always been great to work with. He charges top dollar, but you get what you pay for. I'll own that Roadster for the rest of my life, it will last forever. He took the best of the old and the new and combined it into the perfect hot rod. The trouble is, I'm hooked now and I'll have to go back on tour if I want another car. ∎

57

Above: No fuel-injected Corvette motor here. Instead, it's a very traditional 350 with a carburetor. Left: Three-piece aluminum hood was formed by Marcel's, squirted by Greg Morrell and flamed and striped by Dennis Ricklefs.

The windshield posts, billet aluminum products from Boyds, support a pair of rear view mirrors and flank a flat glass windshield. The only other modification to the body consisted of the installation of electronically operated taillights and license plate which only roll down and become visible when the motor is turned on. When the motor is off, the whole assembly is neatly tucked out of sight.

The simple but effective tomato red leather interior (more homage to Mexican food?) with tasteful tuck n' roll inserts was the work of Gabe Lopez and features a billet aluminum instrument panel fitted with three VDO gauges, comprising speedo, water temp and fuel, a Boyds pedal set, a Boyds leather wrapped "Cushion Grip" Ultra Classic steering wheel atop a modified GM tilt column and billet aluminum door handles milled to match the steering wheel.

So far, we've mentioned everything but the stereo and you can't imagine a bass master like Van Halen's Michael not having one. Sure enough, every bit of unseen space, under and behind the seats and in the trunk is jammed with a serious Pioneer system coupled to Orion speakers and amps.

There remains but two items to talk about. The first, and most obvious, is the paint. Designed by Chip, the "Hard Rock Black" DuPont was applied by Greg Morrell while the pearl white, orange and red with green striping flames were laid down by master flamer/striper Dennis Ricklefs.

Finally, there's the hardtop, designed to be easily removable and give this flamin' star of the Southern California freeway system the ability and comfort of being an all-year driver, especially when used in conjunction with the fully integrated, but well hidden air conditioning system.

Fred Warren/DuPont
SMOOTHSTER

Despite his heavy work load as a chief designer at Chevrolet, Hot Rods by Boyd had the pleasure of working with the Aluma Coupe/CadZZilla designer Larry Erickson once again, along with CadZZilla fabricator Craig Naff on yet another significant project and AMBR winner, Fred Warren's DuPont Smoothster.

Craig had left Hot Rods by Boyd after his work on CadZZilla and moved back to Woodstock, Virginia, where he had been contacted by Robbie Midollo, the original owner of what became the Smoothster, who wanted Craig to hot rod him a '37 Ford cabriolet.

"He had three things in mind when he commissioned Craig to build him a car," recalls Erickson. "He liked the looks of a '37 Ford, but wanted it smoothed over. And, while he wanted it low—very low—he also wanted to be able to drive it and drive it hard."

As Hot Rods by Boyd has found with other projects that require extensive body reworking, it is often easier to build a completely new car than modify an existing one. And so it was that Craig called in Larry who, "Began designing a completely new car from the inside out, and set up an interior package that was large and roomy with a lot of attention paid to the seating position, the location of the controls and the placement of the steering column and instrument cluster."

Once the packaging requirements had been decided, Larry laid out a full-size side view which, according to Larry, "Retained the spirit of the '37 Ford, captured the character, if you like, but was not a literal translation."

Everything else was scaled from the full-size and Craig began work on the chassis using a pair of Just-A-Hobby rails suspended on then current Corvette independent front and rear suspension, complete with brakes, springs, shocks and rack-and-pinion steering. The motor was likewise Corvette, being a '92 LT1 mated to a 700R4 transmission.

With the basic mechanical components positioned, Craig con-

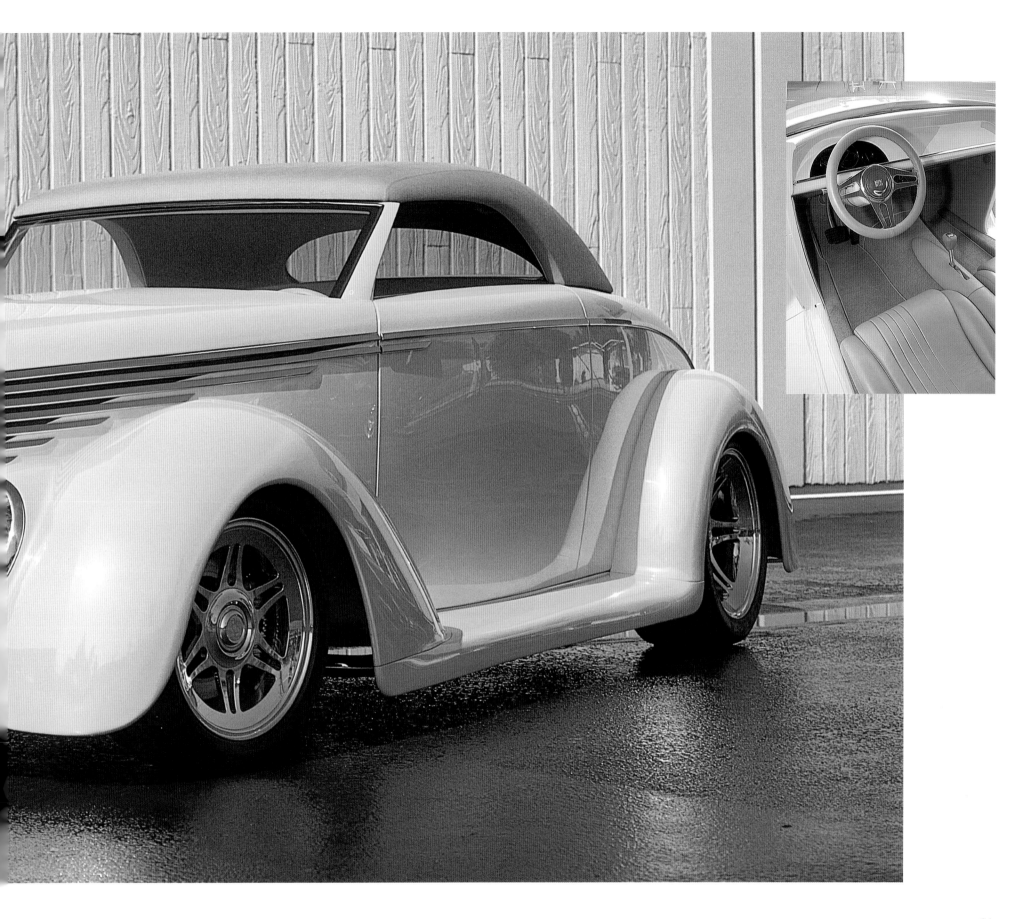

Above: The fabrication of any one-off body, such as that built by Craig Naff for Fred Warren's DuPont Smoothster, begins with a wooden buck which forms the dimensional base upon which the body panels are fitted. As you can see, a great deal of ground work is necessary before a car of this caliber can be completed. It's not work for the faint of heart. (Photo courtesy of Larry Erickson.)
Right: Even when all the metal is hammered smooth there remains a great deal of body work and detailing to complete before Greg Morrell and Keith Russell are able to apply one of those signature Hot Rods by Boyd paint jobs.

structed a wooden buck over which he formed an aluminum body. At that time Larry put in a lot of miles between his home in Detroit and Craig's shop in order to get the key points of the body character exactly right. Other original old Fords in Craig's shop provided good reference.

Because of its resistance to "road rash," steel rather than aluminum was used in the fabrication of the recessed floor pan, fenders and running boards. One interesting and unusual detail of the car is the power-brake booster molded into the firewall. Usually these items are hidden rather than be made a feature. Craig also put in a lot of time installing electric windows and fabricating a folding top when, unfortunately, Midollo had to step away from the project. Knowing who could finish the car, Craig put a call into Boyd and it wasn't long before it came to Hot Rods by Boyd.

Although much had been done, much remained to do. For example,

Hot Rods by Boyd removed the electric windows, rolled the tops of the doors and turned the car into a roadster. The folding top was similarly discarded in favor of a Carson-style removable padded hardtop. Meanwhile, Larry's original design had called for 15- and 16-inch wheels. However, Boyds Wheels wanted to debut some new 17- and 18-inch wheels so the wheel wells were opened up—not a simple task—and Boyds Wheels machined up some 220-pound chunks of billet aluminum to which were attached 7- and 10-inch rims. The fax machines of Chip Foose, Boyd's chief designer, and Larry were red hot as the date of the 1995 Oakland Roadster Show grew near.

The one major task that still lay ahead was the formation of the art deco-style grille which comprised 66 hand-contoured beveled-edge $^3/_4$ x $^3/_8$-inch solid brass straps that were shaped by George Gould and block-sanded smooth by Chip before being chrome plated.

Once the grille, the top bar of which forms the belt line, sweeping all the way to the rear of the body, was ready for plating, the whole vehicle was disassembled for final detailing. The forged aluminum Corvette suspension parts were ground smooth by Pete Morrell and painted in DuPont semi-gloss Champagne pearl metallic by his brother Greg, who with Keith Russell, prepared the body parts for shooting in DuPont "Boyd Yellow."

January 1995 saw Fred Warren's DuPont Smoothster roll into Oakland to immediately become one of the "all-time" rods which certainly stands the test of time, looking as good today as it did when it picked up "the big one" for America's Most Beautiful Roadster, a true credit to the team and the effort of everybody involved. ⬤

Fred Warren on Hot Rods by Boyd

've been doing this hot rod thing since I was 14. I can remember driving back and forth to high school when I was just a kid in a '29 Roadster when everybody else had their moms and dads dropping them off. Back then, I never would have dreamed about having a car built by somebody of Boyd's caliber, but eventually I traded a Deuce roadster I had built for a Boyd car and it was just outstanding. The car was so neat and so sound and so different from what I was used to. Boyd's cars just have a certain quality and look that you don't find anywhere else. And, after I got more successful with my business, this is where I decided to go to have my cars built..

Of course, I'd known about his work since he was at his garage. Later, I started coming out to California and would visit him in the old building on Monroe Avenue. That's about the time I started buying cars that he'd built and it's progressed to where he builds almost all my cars.

I used to buy and trade and sell a lot, but without a doubt, the Smoothster is my favorite. That car was a gigantic hit, great for him and great for me. I'd like to think it helped elevate Hot Rods by Boyd to a higher level of visibility. I will probably keep that car forever and if I did decided to sell it, I promised Boyd I'd sell it back to him. The truth is, I don't sell them anymore because I really don't like to stand there with a bag of money while somebody is running off with two years of my creative work.

Fred Warren's DuPont Smoothster much as it arrived at Hot Rods by Boyd from Craig Naff. Much done but much to do. (Photo courtesy of Eric Geisert and *Street Rodder* magazine.)

Having retired I now have the wherewithal to do this type of thing and I still enjoy it as though I was a sixteen-year-old kid. When I go to Oakland and sit in on the Hall of Fame, it makes the hair on my neck stand up. So we just keep coming back for more. I still build a few rods myself. They're okay, but I build, shall we say, less complicated cars. My shop is not nearly as big as Boyd's but I have a full machine shop and a paint booth and room for two trucks and trailers and 14 cars.

The last car that I built that was an all-out hot rod was the 1996 sweep-stakes winner at the Houston Grand Finale—it's been a very successful car, but I don't have the metal working talents and the benefit of Chip, who is one of my all-time favorite people. He has become a very good friend of mine. So he designs 'em, Boyd's guys build 'em and we go have fun with 'em.

Right now we're building a brand new concept that Chip designed when he was at Art Center College of Design, Pasadena, California. He was kind enough to let me build a roadster version of his coupe. Mine will be front-engined but I kind of let him decide how he wants to build it. We're looking to debut the car in February 1998 in Detroit where we're going to put it in contention for the Riddler Award. We're looking to finish the car early January so I can do some things to it myself at my shop.

We're also building a '33 coupe. The concept came about when Chip and Boyd and I were talking one day and I said I'd like to build a nineties version of the Vern Luce Coupe. They said, "Yeah, we can do that." Well, I had this original body back home, which I thought was pretty good but obviously wasn't as good as I thought it was. John Buttera calls it my billet coupe because they've almost rebuilt the whole car—which is fine. When it's finished it will be a piece of art.

We've changed our direction slightly because while it will be a hi-boy '33 three-window coupe, we're not trying to clone Vern's car, it will definitely be a nineties hot rod with late-model powertrain, high-tech suspension and 20-inch wheels. It will stand on its own and we plan on debuting that car in August 1997 at the Goodguys Pleasanton event.

Those two projects will keep me going for a while and thankfully my wife Patti is very understanding and supports me in this.

Over the years, I've gotten to know Boyd to be a very private person, I think he selects his friends very carefully and I'd liked to be counted as one of them, which I think I am. ■

Above: The injector cover, painted "Chip Silver" to match the LT1 Corvette block and drivetrain components, is typical of how Hot Rods by Boyd detail their engines. Not so typical is the molding of the power-brake booster into the firewall.

Left: Beautiful hand-formed art-deco-style grille was designed by Larry Erickson and made from 66 beveled-edge $3/4$ x $3/8$ solid brass bars by George Gould. Chip Foose block-sanded each bar before chrome plating. (Photo courtesy of Bo Bertilsson.)

Above right: Upon arrival at the 1995 Oakland Roadster Show, hence the missing and taped hub caps, the Smoothster gets ready to knock 'em dead. Incidentally, the exhausts are tucked up out of sight under the running boards.

Specifications

Owner:	Fred Warren	Column:	Modified GM	Manufacturer:	Craig Naff/ Hot Rods by Boyd	Paint materials:	DuPont
Designer:	Larry Erickson	Engine block:	'92 Corvette LT1	Material:	Aluminum	Color:	Boyd Yellow
		Induction:	Fuel injection	Hood:	Aluminum	Painter:	Greg Morrell
Chassis type:	'37 Ford perimeter	Driveshaft:	Custom	Cowl:	Steel		
Builder:	Craig Naff	Transmission:	700R4	Grille:	66 bevel-edged	Upholsterer:	Jim Griffin
Rails:	Just-A-Hobby	Shifter:	Gennie		3/4 x 3/8-inch	Material:	Leather
					solid brass bars	Color:	Tan
Front suspension:	Corvette IFS	Front wheels:	Boyds Smoothster		hand-formed by	Carpet:	Tweed
Shocks:	Corvette		16 x 7		George Gould	Material:	Wool
Brakes:	Corvette	Front tires:	BFGoodrich	Front fenders:	Hand-formed steel	Color:	Tan
			205/45ZR-16	Rear fenders:	Hand-formed steel	Seats:	Reworked Corvette
Rear suspension:	Corvette IRS	Rear wheels:	Boyds Smoothster	Doors:	Hand-formed	Material:	Leather
Shocks:	Corvette		18 x 10		aluminum	Color:	Tan
Brakes:	Corvette	Rear tires:	BFGoodrich	Trim:	Hand-formed brass	Steering wheel:	Boyds Ultra Classic
Differential:	Corvette		295/35ZR-18	Windshield:	Cut down Corvette	Instrument panel:	Custom
				Top:	Carson-style	Instruments:	VDO
Master cylinder:	Corvette	Gas tank:	Custom	Front lights:	'37 Ford	Audio head unit:	Sony
				Rear:	Tear-drop style,	Speakers:	Orion
Steering:	Rack-and-pinion	Body style:	'37 Roadster		hand-formed by	Installation:	Stereo Bob
Rack:	Corvette				Chip Foose		

Ed Burden
'53 STUDEBAKER

Above left: Sparse, race-car-inspired interior is all business with its full roll-cage, Momo seats, Boyds wheel, Classic Instruments and Hurst-shifted Doug Nash five-speed. (Photos courtesy of Petersen Publishing.)

Typically, a hot rod by Boyd is like a baby, it has a gestation period of about 9 months. Occasionally, however, for various reasons, they take a little longer to see the light of day. Take, for example, Ed Burden's '53 Studebaker post coupe.

Ed, who resides in New York where he houses an impressive and diversified car collection, had always wanted a car he could call his own. So, in 1989, he commissioned Boyd to build him a dual-purpose hot rod. "What I was looking for Boyd to do," said Ed, "was combine the classic Euro-American look of Raymond Loewy's '53 Studebaker Champion with the no-nonsense performance of a NASCAR stocker. But, what I definitely didn't want was a Pro Stocker."

A good clean car was subsequently found in California and work began at the Monroe Avenue shop where Darwin "Squeek" White and Tom Garrity chopped the top four inches in the front and two inches in the rear. Meanwhile, Larry Sergejeff fabricated a tubular steel chassis to NHRA specifications while retaining the original Studebaker wheelbase. In typically Hot Rods by Boyd fashion, the chassis sports fully independent suspension at all four corners with Carrera coil-over shocks. The part-built car was featured in the winter 1991 issue of *Custom Rodder*.

To power the beast of Burden, Ray Harstad was chosen to assemble a 454-cubic-inch, all-aluminum Donovan V8, which is mounted solidly, race-car style, to the to the frame, and with a single carburetor under a Boyds air cleaner produces in excess of 500 horsepower.

Unfortunately, as sometimes happens, Ed got sidetracked with other issues and the Studebaker's skeleton was pushed into a closet where it gathered dust for a few years. However, Ed kept seeing other people's Studebakers in the magazines and eventually he called Boyd with instructions to put his project back on the front burner.

Hot Rods by Boyd had, meanwhile, moved to its present location at 10541 Ashdale where in the early part of 1995, the coupe was dusted

off and work resumed—Boyd having promised Ed he would deliver the car in Lincoln, Nebraska, during the *Rod and Custom* Americruise.

The passage of time dictated that some details change. For example, the narrowed nine-inch Ford rear end originally intended for the car was discarded in favor of a Boyd independent rear fitted with a Corvette center section, Carrera coil-over shock absorbers and Wilwood brakes.

The tire and wheel combination mixes 16 x 7 and 17 x 9.5 Vintage IIs from Boyds Wheels shod with BFGoodrich P205/55R16s in front and P255/50R17s in the rear.

Meanwhile, in true hot rod tradition, the body was shaved of handles, script and all extraneous trim and had its rear lights frenched in traditional style before being squirted by Greg Morrell in what became known as "Chip Silver." Inside, all was equally business like with acres of aluminum and a pair of Momo seats surrounded by tubes of steel and faced by a Boyds wheel and a six-pack of Classic Instruments

Above: Photographed here by Gray Baskerville at the Bonneville Salt Flats, this tube-framed Chip-Silver coupe looks right at home. All external chrome, except the bumpers, were removed for that clean, race-car look.

Right: Under the Boyds billet filter and all-aluminum Donovan 454 V8 was balanced and blueprinted by Ray Harstad to produce more than 500 horsepower, pushing Ed Burden's beast to speeds in excess of 150 mph. (Photos courtesy of Petersen Publishing.)

mounted in a painted aluminum dash. It's the bare necessities and that's the way Ed likes it, saying, "I wanted the illusion of being in a race car and its Spartan interior was just perfect. I love the feel of the Doug Nash five-speed. I love the exhaust note which reminded me of my Purolator Merc or one of the Super Stockers in my collection. It was exactly what I had in mind when I called Boyd seven years ago."

True to his word, Boyd had the car ready to deliver on the Americruise, however, chief designer Chip Foose gave the Southern California automotive design community a sneak preview when he rumbled in to an invitation-only car show at Toyota's Newport Beach, California, Calty advanced styling studio and drove away with one of the top awards.

Although it was a long time getting here, when it finally arrived, Burden's beast was true to the name hot rod, being right in stance, loud in sound and capable of exceeding 150 mph.

Specifications

Original owner:	Ed Burden	Steering type:	Fiat rack-and-pinion	Rear tires:	BFGoodrich P255/50R17	Paint materials:	DuPont
		Column:	Modified GM			Color:	Chip Silver
Chassis type:	1¹/₂-inch chrome moly tubular	Engine block:	Solid-mounted Donovan all-aluminum 454	Gas tank:	Fuel cell	Painter:	Greg Morrell
Builder:	Larry Sergejeff			Body style:	'53 "Post" coupe	Interior:	Aluminum panels, full roll cage
		Induction:	Carburetor	Manufacturer:	Studebaker	Carpet:	Black
Front suspension:	Fully independent with tubular steel A-arms	Horsepower:	500 approx.	Modifications:	Chopped three inches in front, five inches in back. Nosed and decked. Door handles shaved. Front pan removed	Material:	Wool
		Builder:	Ray Harstad			Color:	Black
		Transmission:	Doug Nash 5-speed			Seats:	Momo
Shocks:	Carrera coil-over	Shifter:	Hurst			Color:	Black
Brakes:	Wilwood					Steering wheel:	Boyds Ultra Classic
		Front wheels:	Boyds Vintage II 16 x 7			Dashboard:	Aluminum
Rear suspension:	Boyd independent	Front tires:	BFGoodrich P205/55R16			Instruments:	Classic Instruments
Shocks:	Carrera coil-overs			Front lights:	Stock. Headlight bezels painted	Wheelbase:	Stock
Brakes:	Wilwood					Weight:	3,000 pounds approx.
Differential:	Corvette	Rear wheels:	Boyds Vintage II 17 x 9.5	Rear lights:	Frenched		
Master cylinder:	Tilton						

Butch Martino
'51 FORD

As you can read elsewhere in this book, Butch Martino has had a number of cars built by Hot Rods by Boyd including the 1990 Oakland Roadster Show winner and the '34 three-window coupe that appeared on the cover of *Smithsonian* magazine. As Butch points out on page 19, the coupe was much more practical than the roadster but even a coupe can be a little cramped at times and Butch was, "Interested in something different, something other than a street rod."

The car in question, a '51 Ford Victoria, was one of those projects that Boyd was building on spec, knowing that somebody who appreciated the style, the spirit of the modifications and the workmanship would come along. And that somebody was Butch who, as he says, "Saw it finished. Liked it. And we cut a deal."

Externally, the '51 is fairly stock, but underneath the pristine hardtop, the original chassis was subjected to a number of modifications. For example, the rear axle is a nine-inch Ford modified and narrowed by Currie Enterprises and mounted on parallel leaf springs. Up front there is a Mustang II clip from Fat Man Fabrications.

In order to retain the all-Ford theme, Boyds turned to Ford SVO for one of their potent fuel-injected five-liter crate motors which is topped with one of Boyd's signature engine covers painted to match. The engine is coupled to a C-4 auto trans which, incidentally, is controlled by a column-mounted shifter. The column itself is a '78 Chevy van part with modified linkage topped with a Boyds Ultra Classic steering wheel. The dash and instrumentation is all restored stock.

The body modifications, handled by Ralph Kirby, were, in comparison, infinitely more subtle. To begin with, Gene Winfield headlight rims replaced the stock items and were welded solid to the body for that classic custom frenched look. Also, the door handles were shaved along with the hood ornament. However, the grille and bumper remain basically as original. An external remote is used for opening the doors.

The major visual external difference is the use of Chip Foose-

Left: Butch's '51 Victoria and Ed Burden's '53 Studebaker were photographed together for the cover of the February 1996 issue of *Rod and Custom*. We included the left side of the photograph to show that California is not always what it seems. (Photos courtesy of Petersen Publishing.)

designed graphics that emulate the trim of the Ford Crestliner. In this case, however, Chip used an eye-catching combination of DuPont black and what has become known as "Chip Silver" with an orange accent pinstriped by Dennis Ricklefs to define Butch's ride as something different and individual.

The same combination of colors was repeated inside where the stock bench seat was reupholstered by Ron Mangus in black leather and wool to match the Chip Silver paint. With the exception of the steering column and wheel and black-colored Boyds billet pedals, the interior appointments remain stock except for the addition of a Pioneer audio unit backed up by Orion amps and speakers.

As you would expect, Butch's ride rides on Boyds Wheels, in this case it's classic style Vintage IIs shod with BFGoodrich tires.

Above: Butch's '51 Victoria is powered by a fuel-injected Ford SVO five-liter V8 adorned with one of Boyd's signature engine covers, in this case painted "Chip Silver" to match the block and exterior.
Right: Headlight rims from Gene Winfield were frenched into the front fenders, the door handles were shaved, as was the hood, but all the front end chrome is factory fresh. The Chip Foose-designed graphics applied by Greg Morrell and with pinstriping by Dennis Ricklefs, emulate those of a Ford Crestliner while the wheels are Boyds Vintage IIs shod with BFGoodrich rubber.

BOYDSTER

Ever since hot rodders started messin' with Henry Ford's venerable Deuce roadster, they've been trying to smooth out its lumps and bumps, reveals, hinges and hiccups. The problem with the Shiatsu system of heavy massage is that if you take it too far, you're in danger of loosing the very thing that makes a Deuce so appealing in the first place—its character and style which, incidentally, was developed under the guidance of Henry's son, Edsel Ford.

Tradition notwithstanding, it's in a hot rodder's blood to keep tinkering and so it was that Chip and Boyd asked the question, "How clean can you make a '32 Roadster?" Their plan was to get rid of everything unnecessary, retaining only the essentials.

Initially, the Boydster, then unnamed, was to be a shop car that everybody could drive, utilizing an old frame that was kicking around along with a similarly spare fiberglass body. The problem was, neither Chip nor Boyd are big fans of fiberglass— they much prefer the feel of steel. It's easier to work with and it's serviceable. Heck, original Deuce bodies are 65 years old now and still going strong. The decision was made therefore, to go with what's real. While they were at it, though, they decided this would be the ideal opportunity to try to improve upon the original.

Usually, when a one-off car such as the Boydster is built, a scale model will be built from which dimensions are taken. However, in this case, to speed up the build time, a steel wire-frame buck was made. Stock Deuce dimensions were used as a guide but all the lines were manipulated. For example, the rear wheel wells, which were radiussed off the axle center line, were lifted three inches. The body was sectioned 3¹/₄ inches and it was tapered toward the cowl where it is three inches narrower than a stock '32. The grille shell, however, is stock width, to accommodate the Chevrolet engine and Boyd's suspension system, but it was sectioned in the horizontal and vertical planes. In the rear, the body rolls up to meet the roll rear pan.

According to Chip, most of these "tweaks" were "eyeballed." Other styling differences from an original include the lack of a separate cowl, '34-style suicide doors that flow into the laid-back windshield and full-length hood and side panels. A good eye will also notice that the wheelbase has been increased six inches to 112, the same as a '34 Ford.

The buck was subsequently shipped to Marcel De Lay where the body was formed in steel and the hood and decklid in aluminum. Incidentally, the windshield is real glass formed for Boyds by California Glass Bending and is to the same pattern as the Roadstar.

The body was channeled 2¹/₂ inches over a chassis built by Larry

Above left: Nobody could ever accuse Boyd of not being a hard worker. Here he is one Saturday morning turning up the Lil' John-designed hubs for the Boydster. These hubs snap-fit and bolt to the back of the wheel so that there are no lug nuts visible from the outside.

Left: To speed up the construction process, a steel wire frame rather than the usual wooden buck was fabricated as a guide for metalmaster Marcel De Lay. The rear wheel wells were lifted three inches and radiussed of the axle center line and the whole body was sectioned 3¹/₄ inches. The body is also three inches narrower than a stock '32 Ford.

Sergejeff using SAC rails with the '32's telltale reveal now running clear up to the grille instead of turning up at the cowl. The suspension front and rear is traditional Hot Rods by Boyd independent.

Other small structural details which are perhaps less obvious include the oval theme evidenced in the instrument panel, which mirrors the original Ford unit but made in billet aluminum rather than pressed steel, the tiny rear-view mirror molded into the top of the windshield frame, the shift knob and the exhaust tailpipe. The headlights are King Bees fitted with quartz halogen lenses, while the rear light is a full-width custom fabrication. Likewise the three-spoke wheels which were milled by Lil' John Buttera who, at the time, had recently moved under Boyd's wing. With no visible means of support, the wheels are attached to the spindle by a machined hub that snap-fits and bolts to the back of the wheel.

The interior displays equal attention to detail. Leather was dyed red to match the DuPont "Boyd Red" paint. Solenoids for the doors and all switches are tucked out of sight up under the dash and the theme of the upholstery stitched by Gabe Lopez is simple, elegant styling.

Finished with the intention of being Boyd's personal entry in the Oakland Roadster Show for 1996, the Boydster took top honors to become the first of six AMBR wins for Boyd that actually bares his own name.

Many who saw the car at Oakland and the many other shows it has appeared at, could not believe the attention to detail, the fit and finish of the panels and the flawless paint. Also, as they had with Jamie Musselman's Roadster of 15 years prior, they wondered where could street rodding, and the Deuce in particular, go from here. But then they weren't Boyd and Chip and they couldn't conceive of Boydster II—Boyd and Chip could, and did. 🚗

Above right: Marcel and Boyd discuss progress as the Boydster begins to take shape. Notice how the rear pan and decklid differ from an original Deuce Roadster. Right: The grille was sectioned vertically three inches and horizontally.

Specifications

Original owner:	Boyd Coddington	Steering type:	Fiat rack-and-pinion	Manufacturer:	Marcel's/Hot Rods by	Striping:	Dennis Ricklefs
Designer:	Chip Foose	Column:	Modified GM	Boyd		Upholsterer:	Gabriel Lopez
				Material:	Steel	Material/color:	Leather/red
Frame rails:	SAC	Engine block:	'96 Corvette LT1	Hood:	Aluminum "alligator"	Carpet:	Red wool
Builder:	Larry Sergejeff	Transmission:	700R4	Grille:	D.F. Metalworks	Instruments:	Boyds/Classic
Modifications:	Bobbed front horns	Shifter:	Gennie	Grille shell:	Sectioned '32		Instruments
				Doors:	'34-style steel "suic-	Wheel:	Boyds Ultra Classic
Front suspension:	Boyd independent	Front wheels:	Boyds 15 x 7		ide" with solenoids		
Shocks:	Carrera coil-overs	Front tires:	BFGoodrich	Windshield:	California Glass	Audio head:	Pioneer
Brakes:	Wilwood		205/50R15 Euro		Bending:	Amps:	Boyds/Orion
Rear suspension:	Boyd independent		Radial T/A	Front lights:	Sectioned King Bee	Speakers:	Boyds/Orion
Shocks:	Carrera coil-overs	Rear wheels:	Boyds 17 x 9		with PIAA lenses	Installation:	Whistle Stop
Brakes:	Wilwood	Rear tires:	BFGoodrich	Rear:	Custom		
Differential:	Corvette		255/50ZR17	Mirror:	Molded into wind-	Overall length:	141 inches
Ratio:	3.55:1		Comp T/A		shield frame	Overall width:	72 inches
						Overall height:	44 inches
Master cylinder:	Corvette	Body style:	Roadster	Paint:	DuPont "Boyd Red"	Wheelbase:	112 inches
				Painter:	Greg Morrell	Weight:	2,500 pounds

The oval theme is obvious here where you can see the rear-view mirror, instrument panel and exhaust outlet. (Photo courtesy of Scott Williamson.)

Jim Sweeney
'37 FORD

O f the 200 or so cars Hot Rods by Boyd has built in almost 20 years of business, very few of them have been of the '37 Ford variety. There was, of course, Buz Di Vosta's Roadstar which was a concept inspired by the '37 Ford, but there have been few others, that is, until midway through 1996 when the "Sultan of Stanton," as Gray Baskerville nicknamed Boyd, completed work on a '37 Cabriolet for Jim Sweeney of San Diego, California.

Rare in their own right, '37 Cabriolets, especially a Boyd-built one, is truly one of a kind. To begin with, the lid was lowered two inches while the hood was shaved of all unnecessary chrome. Incidentally, the hood is now opened by an inside pull-handle. Likewise shaved were the door handles and the decklid.

Completing the smooth appearance necessitated the removal of both front and rear bumpers and the subsequent filling of all bumper iron holes. The stock rubber-coated running boards were similarly eighty-sixed in favor of smooth, black-painted boards.

Other bodily details include frenched taillights and license plate in the rear and that masterful hand-formed stainless steel grille up front. When Jim paid for the grille, its maker, Ron Covell, said, "Thanks, I appreciate the opportunity and the money but I never want to have to make another." Nevertheless, Ron's workmanship is faultless.

Underneath the exquisite body is a stock Ford chassis upgraded from its original buggy spring suspension in typical Hot Rods by Boyd fashion. In the front it's the ubiquitous independent system with Carrera coil-over shocks, Fiat rack-and-pinion steering and disc brakes. In the rear there's a Corvette center section with in-board discs and, once again, coil-over suspension.

Power is provided by the popular Chevrolet LT1 resplendent in

"Chip Silver" with black detailing, stainless steel headers and a K&N filter. Jim, in search of a little more power, added an NOS nitrous system. Incidentally, the firewall is so flat and shiny that at first glance it looks like the engine bay houses two motors.

Designed, as was the exterior paint scheme, by Chip Foose, the interior, stitched by Gabe Lopez, mirrors the outside being a combination of dark and light gray leather with a simple separation of orange piping. The instrument panel, which complements the Boyds pedals, is a polished full-width billet aluminum item that looks right at home in this 60-year-old car even with its aluminum air conditioning vents and Sony XR 7180 head unit.

The instruments: VDO speedo, fuel, battery, water temperature and oil pressure gauges are tucked neatly behind the modified GM column which is topped with a leather-wrapped three-spoke Boyd wheel. The gray wool carpets are also edged in gray leather.

Finally, as you would expect, Jim's darkly subtle Cabriolet rides on Boyds Vintage II wheels shod with BFGoodrich Radial T/As.

Right: Jim Sweeney's '37 Cabriolet under construction where you can clearly see Boyd's IFS adapted to the '37 chassis. Left: LT1 motor has NOS. Below: Nearing completion, Jim's car shares space with Butch Martino's '34 and Dan Kruse's LT5 Corvette-powered Deuce Roadster.

Above: Gabe Lopez stitched up this beautiful two-tone leather interior which features a full-width billet aluminum instrument panel fitted with VDO gauges and Sony audio unit.

Above: Shaved of all its extraneous lumps and bumps, like the hood ornament, door handles and bumpers, and with black and "Chip Silver" two-tone paint, Jim's '37 takes on a contemporary look. However, the piece de resistance is the hand-formed stainless steel grille which was the work of Ron Covell.

Buz Di Vosta
SPORTSTAR

Top: Photographed here by Randy Lorentzen, Chip and Mark Vaughn of *AutoWeek* magazine put the Sportstar through its paces at a test track outside Los Angeles. Above: From any angle, Sportstar is a metal work of art. The rear lights, like most everything else, were hand-formed. Notice also, the illuminated Lexus instruments.

W hen Mark Vaughn, west coast editor of *AutoWeek* magazine, said, "It looks a little like the back half of a 1957 Corvette melded perfectly with the front half of a 1957 Ferrari Testa Rossa," he wasn't completely wrong. But then, he wasn't completely right, either.

While many people try to find styling queues in the Sportstar from myriad classic sports cars of the past, the Sportstar is all of the above, and yet, paradoxically, none of the above. Yes, the pontoon fenders are reminiscent of Ferrari's legendary red head racer, perhaps the tail hints at a fifties Corvette, but then again, it reminds some of an Austin Healey. And then there's the grille: An homage in stainless steel to Henry Ford's Model 40 if ever there was one. The most sensible answer to this conundrum is, of course, to view the car for what it is, an example of the car as art—the art of the carrozzeria.

As Mark went on to say in that July 29, 1996, cover story, "After 17 years reiterating the basic American hot rod, Coddington Enterprises has branched out, reinvented itself, and, once again, started a new direction for automotive design. Now Coddington and all 350 of the employees who make up his companies have evolved fully from rod and custom makers into coachbuilders."

Anybody who was lucky enough to spend time in Chip's lofty studio which overlooks the grey and white checkered final assembly area of Hot Rods by Boyd, where mops flick constantly back and forth like crazed windshield wipers, might have seen the preliminary sketches for Sportstar thumb tacked to the wall. In fact, Chip had originally penned the concept as a student while attending Art Center College of Design, Pasadena, California. "I was just free-form thinking," said Chip. "Just playing around. Asking myself questions like, 'What else can you do with fenders?' and taking off from the '57 Testa Rossa which had the pontoon fenders and just playing with that theme. That's where it came from."

Three years would pass before the project would take on a third dimension and Chip was able to render it in model form. At that stage, Sportstar became a little more defined as you see it now. Inspiration for the grille actually came from the '33 or '34 Ford, however, Carroll Shelby's legendary Cobra provided inspiration for the back end.

With such an untraditional appearance and having worked with a

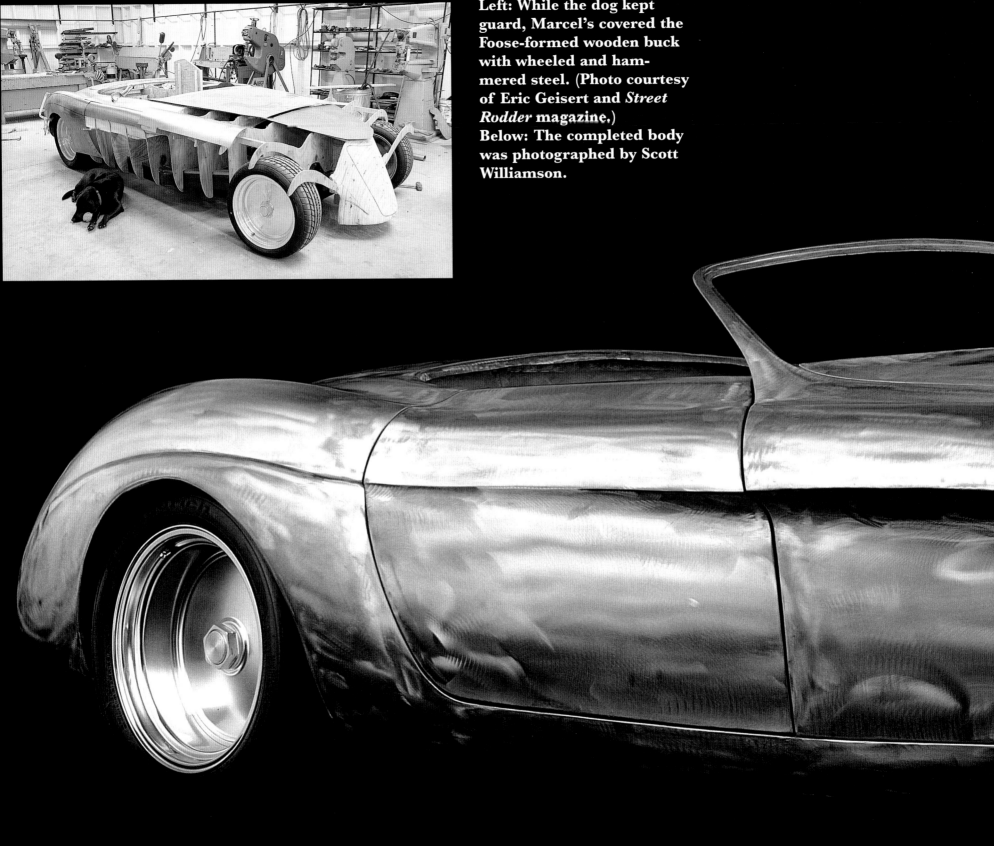

Left: While the dog kept guard, Marcel's covered the Foose-formed wooden buck with wheeled and hammered steel. (Photo courtesy of Eric Geisert and *Street Rodder* magazine.)
Below: The completed body was photographed by Scott Williamson.

Right: Painter par excellence, Greg Morrell blocks out the primer before applying liberal coats of Boyd Red. Ably assisted by Keith Russell, they always seem to pull off the perfect paint job. And the underside of those fenders is just as smooth at the topside.

Above left: Red on red interior features Lexus instrumentation, tilt column fitted with Boyds Tri-grip billet steering wheel and Lexus automatic transmission.
Above right: Chip Foose-designed, Larry Sergejeff-fabricated front suspension consists of Indy car-style A-arms and push-rod operated, cantilevered in-board coil-over shocks.
Right: 260 horsepower, four-cam, 32-valve Lexus V8 was squirted Boyd Red and made to work electronically within the new configuration by Peter Morrell.
(Photos courtesy of Randy Lorentzen.)

from box-section steel tubing. The independent front suspension consists of unequal length billet aluminum A-arms with in-board cantilevered coil-over shocks. In the rear, it's a similar system, however, huge blanks of billet aluminum were hogged out on the mill to form the upper and lower H-section control arms. Again, coil-over shocks form the nucleus of the suspension.

The frame, complete with exhausts and catalytic converters, was shipped out to Marcel De Lay where Chip began forming the wooden buck over which Marcel's would fabricate the steel body. Buck building is a skilled art and a great deal of time and effort went into this stage of the build before Marcel and his sons could begin wheeling up the steel panels. Nevertheless, the spring of '96 saw the project move rapidly forward as Boyd set a date for the unveiling.

Back in Stanton, the body and chassis went immediately to the fabrication shop where Roy Schmidt and Steve Greninger began work detailing the body. Meanwhile, in the chassis shop, Andy Wallin worked on the installation of the pedal assembly, brake system and other chassis components.

With all of the major work completed in just a matter of weeks, the body and chassis went to the paint shop where Greg Morrell and Keith Russell got to work smoothing things out and applying the DuPont Boyd Red paint. Then it was back to fabrication where a new 260-horsepower, four-cam, 32-valve Lexus V8 and four-speed automatic transmission, which had both been squirted gray, were installed in the chassis and hooked up.

Modern computer-controlled powertrains can often cause car builders problems, but Peter Morrell had no problems making the computer understand the new configuration. He was even able to retain the Lexus instrumentation which, when it illuminates the wide and otherwise clear dash, defines Sportstar as a truly modern sports car.

For the interior, Boyd and Chip once again chose the simple and effective combination of red on red. The seats sit astride a tall but narrow transmission tunnel broken only by a leather-clad Lexus shift lever. At 78 inches wide, there's plenty of elbow room. Red carpet, red leather door panels and a red leather wrapped Boyds Tri-Grip steering wheel complete the picture.

Sportstar rides on what was at the time a unique set of wheels. Typically, Boyds Wheels employ billet or cast aluminum centers machined in two planes, however, the Sportstar's star-themed wheels were cut using a new three-dimensional milling machine. Each wheel center took more than five hours to mill before it could be welded into the spun-aluminum rim. Mounted onto those wheels are BFGoodrich Comp T/A radials measuring 205/ZR-17 in front and 315/35ZR-17 in the rear.

variety of modern powerplants, Boyd was searching for an unusual V8 to power Sportstar when he bumped into Brian Bergsteinsson who, at the time, was vice president of Lexus SUVs and trucks, at the North American International Auto Show in Detroit. Brian, a hot rodder with a '39 Ford convertible, was intrigued and decided that Lexus needed to be involved with the project and made available an entire Lexus SC400 powertrain.

Work began in earnest in 1995 when the Larry Sergejeff, using a mock-up motor and transmission, fabricated a perimeter-type frame

Ron Craft
'33 ROADSTER

The day after setting up the Boydster in that hallowed hall of fame, the Oakland Coliseum, at the 1996 Oakland Roadster Show, when most people are breathing a sigh of relief after all the hard work getting there, patting themselves on the back and wondering where they'll find room for that "ginormous" AMBR trophy, Boyd Coddington and Chip Foose were already planning their next collaboration.

In just an incredible five weeks from the moment the Boydster became America's 47th Most Beautiful Roadster, the new car, "Simply Red," and designed for Ron Craft of Texas, was already a rolling chassis with a completely hand-fabricated body, about to go into the paint shop.

Let's back up though. Chip's original sketches called for styling that takes its queues: the full-length hood and side panels, the '34-style suicide doors, and the wraparound windshield, from the cowl-less Boydster and transfers them to the more curvaceous and fluid lines of Henry Ford's 1933-'34 Model 40. To say the modifications work would be an understatement and Ron's Roadster, known simply as "Simply Red," has become yet another testament to the craftsmanship of the team at Hot Rods by Boyd.

As usual, Larry Sergejeff assembled the heavily tapered chassis using SAC rails and tubular crossmembers. In this case, however, the independent suspension would take on a different appearance from that of the Boydster and the shocks would be mounted in-board instead of out in the breeze for all to see.

In the rear, the Koni coil-overs are mounted atop and parallel to the rear crossmember, right above the Corvette differential, and are actuated by bell-cranks and pushrods mounted to the hub carriers. In the front, it's a similar story: the Koni shocks are mounted behind the polished stainless steel D. F. Metalworks grille and are likewise actuated by bell cranks and pushrods. The assembly, both front and rear, not only looks sanitary, but also works exceptionally well.

Left: The first direct descendent of the Boydster was this '33 Roadster built in the same style originally for Ron Craft. "Simply Red," as it was sometimes called, featured another all-steel body with aluminum hood top and side panels hand-formed by Marcel De Lay. To the untrained eye, the grille shell might look like any other '33 Ford shell. However, a closer inspection reveals that it is a hand-formed shell wherein the bottom is similar to that of a '32, but peaked, and the top is similar to a '33 but has tighter radii in the back corners and the nose is pulled down and pancaked. Below: Gabe Lopez stitched the "Boyd Red" interior.

As soon as Larry had completed a rolling chassis, it was shipped out to Marcel De Lay where he and his two sons, Marc and Luc, working only from Chip's full-size side view rendering and a wire-frame buck similar to that employed in the construction of the Boydster, quickly wheeled up a new steel body complete with moldings, a deck lid, windshield frame and a floor. Marcel's also fabricated the full-length aluminum hood and side panels to conform to the laid-back grille shell.

To the untrained eye, the grille shell, which is actually mounted to the hood top and consequently lifts with the hood, looks like any other '33 Ford shell. But a closer inspection reveals that in fact this is actually a hand-formed shell wherein the bottom is similar to that of a '32 Ford rather than a Model 40 but peaked. The top is similar to a '33 but has tighter radii in the back corners whereas the nose is pulled down and pancaked. The shell was also laid back until, as Chip says, "It looked right."

In just a few weeks, the body was completed and the car was back in Stanton where is was primed and Karl Jonasson and Andy Wallin began the mock-up assembly. Under the hood is the ubiquitous Corvette LT1 motor, 700R4 transmission, Corvette master cylinder with power booster and modified GM steering column.

Once the mock-up was complete, the whole car was torn apart for paint and chrome and while Chip's original rendering had called for bright yellow paint, the choice was made to go for Boyd Red. And, as you can see, almost everything, with the exception of those parts directly behind the grille, which are black, and the polished stainless steel exhaust, were painted or plated.

For the interior Boyd and Chip chose to match the exterior color exactly by having the leather dyed to match. The excellent work is that of Gabriel Lopez who wrapped his red-dyed skins around a hand-formed bench seat that flows into sweeping door panels which disappear under the smooth wraparound dash. Boyds pedals, a Tri-Grip Boyds billet steering wheel and Classic Instruments in a Boyds billet dash, complete the cockpit.

Again, there was a deviation from the original artwork in the choice of wheels and instead of the tri-spoke design, Boyds Wheels machined up a very special set of exposed lug five spokers which have neither been named nor duplicated.

Since its completion, Ron's roadster has walked away with the prestigious Millwinder Award at its first major showing at the 1996 Houston Autorama where it also won awards for Best Rod and Best Display. Incidentally, Ron was a previous recipient of the Millwinder Award.

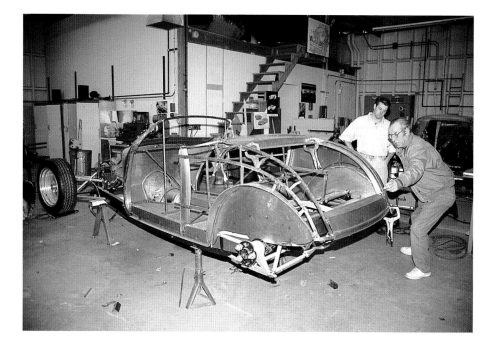

Top: Chip, left, and Marcel De Lay review the progress of construction over a steel wire-frame buck.
Above: To enable a really clean look to the front end, Chip's design called for cantilever-operated in-board shocks which in the front are mounted behind the D. F. Metalworks stainless steel grille. In the rear, they sit horizontally above the rear crossmember. Notice how far the grille is laid back.

The question one asks when viewing this photograph of the Vern Luce Coupe, Jamie Musselman's Roadster and a naked "Simply Red" is, "What's next?"

Specifications

Original owner:	Ron Craft	Differential:	Corvette	Body style:	Roadster	Striping:	Dennis Ricklefs
Designer:	Chip Foose	Ratio:	3.55:1	Manufacturer:	Marcel's/		
					Hot Rods by Boyd	Upholsterer:	Gabriel Lopez
Chassis type:	Perimeter	Master cylinder:	Corvette	Material:	Steel	Material/color:	Leather/Boyd Red
Frame rails:	SAC			Doors:	Steel "suicide" with	Carpet material	
Builder:	Larry Sergejeff	Steering:	Fiat rack-and-pinion		solenoids	/color:	Wool/Boyd Red
		Column:	Modified GM	Hood:	Aluminum "alligator"	Instruments:	Boyds/Classic
Front suspension:	Independent with			Grille:	D.F. Metalworks		Instruments
	cantilever in-board	Engine block:	'96 Corvette LT1	Grille shell:	Hand formed	Steering wheel:	Boyds Tri-Grip
	shocks	Transmission:	700R4			Pedals:	Boyds
Shocks:	Koni coil-over	Shifter:	Gennie	Windshield:	California Glass		
Brakes:	Wilwood				Bending	Head unit:	Pioneer
		Front wheels:	Boyds 16 x 7			Amps:	Boyds/Orion
Rear suspension:	Independent with	Front tires:	BFGoodrich	Front lights:	Sectioned King Bee	Speakers:	Boyds/Orion
	horizontally opposed		205/50R16 Euro		with PIAA lenses	Installation:	Whistle Stop
	cantilever in-board		Radial T/A	Rear lights:	Custom		
	shocks	Rear wheels:	Boyds 17 x 9.5	Mirror:	Molded into wind-	Overall length:	147 inches
Shocks:	Koni coil-over	Rear tires:	BFGoodrich		shield frame	Overall width:	72 inches
Brakes:	Wilwood		255/50ZR17 Comp			Overall height:	44 inches
			T/A	Paint materials:	DuPont	Weight:	2,500 pounds
		Gas tank:	Custom	Color:	Boyd Red	Wheelbase:	116 inches
				Painter:	Greg Morrell		

BOYDSTER II

If the Boydster, the winner of America's Most Beautiful Roadster (AMBR) award at the 1996 Oakland Roadster Show, was indeed a beautiful hot rod, then surely, with the Boydster II, Boyd and Chip took the concept to its natural conclusion. Conceived by Chip and Boyd while they attended the aforementioned show, work began on Boydster II and Ron Craft's similarly styled '33 Roadster (see page 90) almost immediately upon the duo's return to Stanton.

Chip began, as usual, by generating a full-size side view rendering. This time, however, the body was sectioned two inches and would be channeled only ¹/₂-inch over the frame rails—subtle but nevertheless significant differences from its precursor. More obvious are the steel fenders and running boards which, unlike those on most full fendered Deuce Roadsters

From any angle the Boydster II is an incredibly beautiful automobile and a credit to the craftsmanship of the team at Hot Rods by Boyd. (Photos courtesy of Scott Killeen and Petersen Publishing right, and Scott Williamson below.)

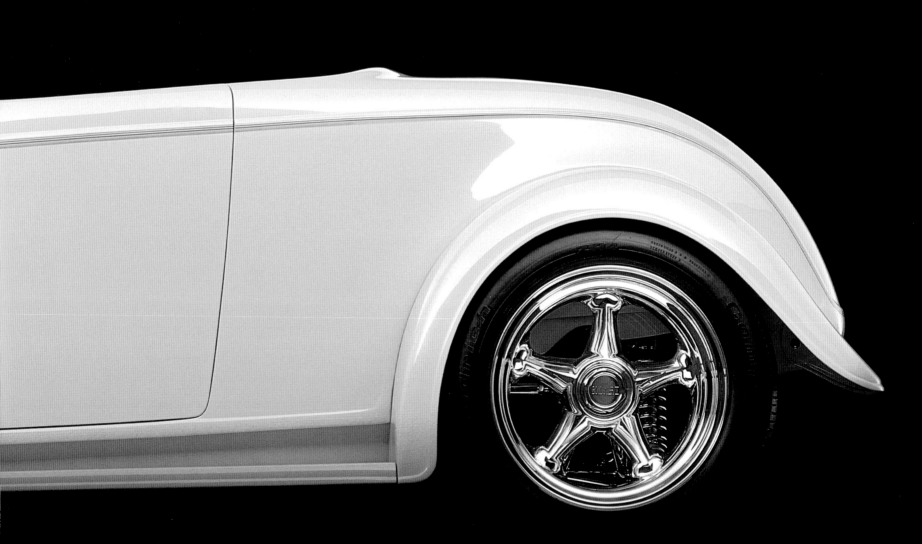

Right: This full-size rendering of the Boydster II and a rolling chassis is all the reference that was given to Marcel De Lay and his sons Marc and Luc before they started work wheeling and hammering the steel and aluminum.
Below right: Steve Greninger, one of Boyd's talented craftsmen works on the installation of an oval rear view mirror.
Opposite page, top left: At one point '34-style skirted fenders were tried but they were not to be.
Opposite page, top right: Pete Morrell where he can usually be found, tucked up under the dash handling the wiring.

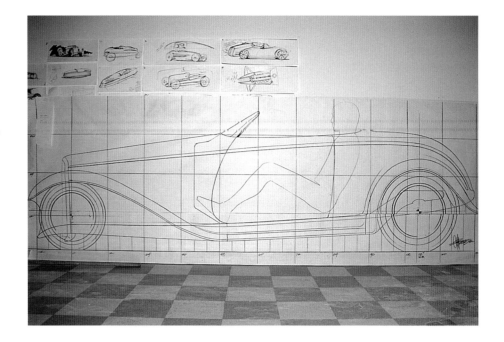

are mounted on the side rather than under the chassis rails which, incidentally, were fabricated by SAC.

Because of the placement of the running boards, Boydster II does not have the traditional strengthening reveal stamped into the side of the rail and yet exactly the same amount of frame is exposed due to the reduced channel.

Once the design was finalized the rendering was handed on to Marcel's where Chip Foose formed a new wooden buck from which they created another all-steel body. The "alligator" hood and hood sides were made of aluminum and the Brookville grille shell was sectioned in exactly the same way as was the Boydster to accept a D. F. Metalworks polished stainless steel grille insert.

Though unveiled at the 1996 SEMA Show, well in time for the 1997 Oakland Roadster Show, Boyd decided not to enter the competition. Nevertheless, those at Hot Rods by Boyd were extremely pleased when Petersen Publishing wanted to photograph it for both *Hot Rod* and *Rod and Custom* magazines.

Rain, sickness and scheduling problems delayed the shoot almost to the Christmas vacation, stretching the window of opportunity because the car was due to go on tour right after the holiday. Yet everybody came together one glorious dawn at Castaic Lake, north of Los Angeles.

It was "deja view" for Gray "Yer ol' Dad" Baskerville and Hot Rods by Boyd because one of the locations chosen by photographer Scott Killeen was Templeton Highway—the very same piece of road where Petersen had photographed Boyd driving Jamie Musselman's roadster, his first AMBR winner, back in 1982 for the cover of *Hot Rod* magazine. Hot Rods by Boyd has come a long way in those ensuing 15 years.

During the day-long shoot, which involved a great deal of action photography, the Boydster II performed flawlessly as Gray hammered it up and down the highway while Scott, lashed to the roof of his van, snapped the shutter. ◆

Left: Sectioned King Bee headlights are fitted with PIAA lenses. Grille was hand-formed by Dan Fink. Far left: Gray Baskerville sneaks behind the wheel one more time. (Scott Killeen photo courtesy of Petersen Publishing.) Below: Interior of Boydster II is bright but simple and elegant. Features include Boyds/Classic Instruments gauges, Boyds pedals, Tri-Grip steering wheel and Gennie shifter. Leather was stitched by Gabe Lopez.

Specifications

Original owner:	Boyd Coddington	Steering:	Fiat rack-and-pinion	Material:	Steel	Painter:	Keith Russell
Designer:	Chip Foose	Column:	Modified GM	Modifications:	Sectioned 2 inches	Striping:	Dennis Ricklefs
				Hood:	Aluminum "alligator"		
Chassis type:	IFS	Engine block:	'96 LT1	Grille shell:	Sectioned Brookville	Upholsterer:	Gabriel Lopez
Frame rails:	SAC	Transmission:	700R4		'32	Material/color:	Leather/yellow
Builder:	Larry Sergejeff	Shifter:	Gennie	Grille insert:	D. F. Metalworks	Carpet material/color:	Wool/yellow
Modifications:	Bobbed front horns			Fenders:	Steel	Instruments:	Boyds/Classic
		Front wheels:	Boyds Sportstar 15 x 7	Doors:	Steel "suicide" with		Instruments
		Front tires:	BFGoodrich		solenoids	Steering wheel:	Boyds Tri-Grip
Front suspension:	Boyds independent		205/50R15				
Shocks:	Carrera coil-over		Euro Radial T/A	Windshield:	California Glass	Head unit:	Pioneer
Brakes:	Wilwood	Rear wheels:	Boyds Sportstar 17 x 9		Bending	Amps:	Boyds/Orion
Rear suspension:	Boyds independent	Rear tires:	BFGoodrich			Speakers:	Orion
Shocks:	Carrera coil-over		255/50ZR17 Comp	Front lights:	Sectioned King Bee	Installation:	Whistle Stop
Brakes:	Wilwood		T/A		with PIAA lenses		
Differential:	Corvette			Rear lights:	Custom LED	Overall length:	150 inches
Ratio:	3.55:1	Gas tank:	Aluminum 15 gallon	Mirror:	Molded into wind-	Overall width:	66 inches
					shield frame	Overall height:	44 inches
Master cylinder:	'96 Corvette	Body style:	Roadster			Weight:	2,500 pounds
		Manufacturer:	Marcel's/Hot	Paint materials:	DuPont	Wheelbase:	116 inches
			Rods by Boyd	Color:	Boyd Yellow		

Left: Careful observation will reveal that although the Boydster and the Boydster II are visually similar, there are many subtle differences. For example, the body of Boydster II was sectioned two inches and was channeled only $1/2$-inch over the frame rails. More obvious are the steel fenders and running boards which, unlike those on most full-fendered Deuce Roadsters, are mounted on the side rather than under the chassis rails which were fabricated by SAC. Also, because of the placement of the running boards, Boydster II does not have the traditional strengthening reveal stamped into the side of the rail and yet exactly the same amount of frame is exposed due to the reduced channel.

The Lil' John Buttera-machined three-spoke wheels on the Boydster are also unusual. Based on a sixties, five-spoke motif, they are attached to the spindle by a machined hub that snap-fits and bolts to the back of the wheel.

Notice also that the rear wheelwells have been raised in the hand-fabricated body and that the outer edge of the tire follows the contour of the wheelwell reveal—it's this attention to detail which makes Hot Rods by Boyd stand out from the crowd.

Larry Donelson
'50 PACKARD

By 1950, the Packard Motor Car Company was in dire financial condition and the introduction, in 1948, of its first all-new, post-war car, the Clipper series 2202/2222, having done nothing to alleviate its problems. The well rounded, "Rubenesque" body style was often referred to as the "inverted bathtub" and looking like a "pregnant elephant." In retrospect, however, it has become a stylish and sought after car, particularly the woody, or Station Sedan, as it was named by Packard.

This particular box rod, built for Larry Donelson of Arizona, dates from 1950 when the series was mildly revamped and christened the "Golden Anniversary" models. They were, however, the last woodys Packard would build before ceasing production in 1958.

Due to a lack of capital for new product development, Packard was always making do and the woody, in Chip Foose's opinion, "Looked unfinished." Although they used genuine Northern Birch wood paneling that was structural only in the tailgate, the wood originally only covered the doors and the window surrounds leaving a gap between the doors and the rear fender exposed. So, when Larry brought his Packard to Hot Rods by Boyd, Chip took the opportunity to finish up what Packard omitted by having Hot Rod Hell of San Diego, California, add wood where it was missing.

The original eight cylinder engines were outdated when new, so a new big-block Chevy V8 was installed along with a 400 Turbo trans and a nine-inch Ford rear axle. In the rear, the stock parallel leaf springs were retained but up front a '76 Camaro front clip was grafted to the original rails. Much of the hook up work at Boyds was handled by Conny Jansson who converted the electrics to 12-volt and converted the original column manual shifter to operate the automatic trans.

While the interior of the car was refurbished but left looking original, even down to the use of stock upholstery and carpet, the addition of a gleaming black Greg Morrell paint job and the extra wood certainly makes Larry's woody one of a kind.

Hot Rod Magazine
'29 ROADSTER

O ver the years, Hot Rods by Boyd has been involved in the building of a number of magazine project cars. And as Gray "Yer ol' dad" Baskerville tells it, "I had just pulled high gear in Boyd's '57 Bel Air as the Sultan of Stanton and I headed toward Peoria, Illinois, the site of *Rod and Custom*'s second annual Americruise. Somehow the conversation drifted to building a simple, straightforward, and somewhat affordable streeter."

Boyd's response was enthusiastic, saying, "You're right. We need to show people how to build basic cars that they can have fun with using repro parts that they can buy easily, mail order if necessary."

Upon arrival in Peoria, Boyd and Gray put together a shopping list for the quintessential hi-boy hot rod, a '29 roadster atop Deuce rails. The reasoning was simple: All the components were readily available, they could be easily assembled without any major fabrication and the car would be a celebration of sorts because the car that set Boyd's direction was, of course, the Silver Bullet (see page 8), a '29 on '32 rails. Besides, thought Gray, it would be a kick to see if the team at Hot Rods by Boyd could apply the Coddington credo to what was basically a box of bits in need of assembly into a fifties-style rod.

The nucleus for this kit rod was a brand new repopped '29 roadster body and pinched '32 frame from Brookville Roadster of Brookville, Ohio, a 302-cubic-inch V8 supplied by Ford SVO, a bucket of bright DuPont orange paint and a set of Boyds Vintage wheels shod with BFGoodrich threads.

The coming together was actually fairly painless with completion taking little more than a few months and with everything up and running in time for the summer season of 1997.

Left: Built to be given away, this '29 on Deuce rails is not that far from the "Silver Bullet." However, this was a much more of a kit rod assembled by Hot Rods by Boyd for *Hot Rod* magazine. Here, some of the team at Boyds (clockwise from the top); Gray Baskerville of *Hot Rod* Magazine, Larry Sergejeff, Greg Morrell and Shawn Barbetta apply the elbow grease.

Above: All-new, all-steel body is the work of Brookville Roadster, as was the frame which is hung with TCI, Magnum, Mullins, Wilwood, Borgeson, Boyds Wheels and BFGoodrich components. (Photos courtesy of Petersen Publishing.)

Specifications

Chassis type:	'32 Ford	Discs:	Wilwood	Column:	Mullins	Front wheels:	Boyds Vintage 15 x 6
Builder:	Brookeville Roadster	Calipers:	Magnum			Front tires:	BFGoodrich T/A
Wheelbase:	106 inches			Engine block:	302 Ford SVO		195/60VR-15
		Rear suspension:		Induction:	780 Holley	Rear wheels:	Boyds Vintage 15 x 10
Front suspension:	Durant single leaf	Shocks:	TCI	Ignition:	Mallory	Rear tires:	BFGoodrich T/A
Tube axle:	Magnum	Differential:	Currie 9-inch Ford	Headers:	Hooker		P275/60R-15
Radius rods/		Ratio:	3.50:1	Exhaust:	Borla stainless steel		
batwings:	TCI			Radiator:	Continental Radiator	Body style:	'29 roadster
Shocks:	TCI	Master cylinder:	TCI			Manufacturer:	Brookville Roadster
				Transmission:	B&Mmodified C4	Material:	Steel
		Steering: type:	Vega	Shifter:	Lokar	Hood:	Marcel's
		Box:	Mullins			Grille insert:	Reproduction

Grille shell:	Brookville '32 Ford	Material:	Leather	
Windshield:	Speedway Motors	Color:	Tan	
		Carpet material:	Wool	
Front lights:	Dietz	Color:	Tan	
Rear lights:	Brookville	Steering wheel:	Original Bell donated	
			by Gray Baskerville	
Paint materials:	DuPont	Instruments:	Boyds/Classic	
Painter:	Greg Morrell		Instruments	
Upholsterer:	Gabe Lopez			
Seat type:	Custom bench made			
	by Gabe Lopez			

Above: Boyd Coddington, surrounded by the team at Hot Rods by Boyd, are gathered amidst the pile of parts that will soon be assembled into the *Hot Rod* Magazine Giveaway Roadster powered by a 5.0L Ford SVO V8.
Above left: Four different views of the Roadster show that even when using what amounts to mail-order parts, Hot Rods by Boyd can assemble a beautifully clean car with exactly the right stance proving that it's not what you use but how you use it that separates the men from the Boyds. (Photos courtesy of Petersen Publishing.)

BOYD AIR

oyd Air came about during one of those typical "what if?" breakfast sessions at Boyd's favorite eatery, The Restaurant Next To The White House. That's where the order of the day is inevitably an egg-white vegetable omelet and perhaps some English muffins smeared with peanut butter. Chip mussed, "What if Chevrolet had been playing with the '59 Impala convertible's proportions two years earlier?" In his usual manner, Boyd said, "Draw it up."

Pretty soon, Chip had some sketches of his concept which turned out to be a sectioned and widened '57 Chevy convertible. Of course, Boyd's response was to say, "Let's build it." And as the old adage goes, If you build it, they will come.

Sure enough, John Dianna, Vice President, Executive Publisher of Petersen's Automotive Performance Group, saw the concept and declared that if Boyd built it for the *Hot Rod* Power Tour, they'd put it on the cover of *Hot Rod*. There was, however, a slight time constraint. The cover of the May 1997 issue of *Hot Rod* had to be shot in February 1997. It was by then November 1996.

Until that point, Boyd Air had been on a slow burner. The cowl section of a '59 Impala convertible, which is eight inches wider than a '57 Chevy, had been obtained, along with a couple of '57 Chevy donor cars. But nothing really was happening until the decision was made to meet the deadline. Then it was dolly to the metal as Steve Greninger and Roy Schmidt hammered the steel over a Larry Sergejeff chassis.

The hefty frame was built from 3 x 5- and 3 x 4- and 3 x 3-inch mild steel tubing varying in thickness from $^1/_8$- to $^1/_4$-inch.

Roy had, of course, worked on CheZoom a couple of years earlier, so he knew what he was in for, but the timetable for this project was critical. The extensive bodywork, which comprises a combination of stock, reproduction and custom-fabricated panels, was assembled with only a full-size side rendering to work from and the flawless finish is a

Right: When he's not behind the camera, Gray Baskerville, who has done so much to publicize the efforts of hot rodders like Boyd, can usually be found behind the wheel of their creations, as he was on this day in February 1997, driving for the photo shoot for the May '97 issue of *Hot Rod* magazine. (Scott Killeen photos courtesy Petersen Publishing.)

Above left: The rusted hulk of a '59 Impala convertible provided little more than the cowl, the base of the windshield and its frame.

Above: With nothing more than a full-size line drawing tacked to the wall, Roy Schmidt and Steve Greninger (shown left) completely fabricated Boyd Air in less than four months. The question on most observer's lips is, "Where do you start?" The car is eight inches wider than a stock '57 Chevy.

Left: Steve Greninger fabricates hinges for the eight-inch wider-than-stock hood. On the rear fenders you can see where they have been marked for moving the wheelwells forward.

Above: A full-size side rendering and a color concept sketch is about all you get. Notice how the wheelwells have been reshaped and shunted forward. Door is also four inches longer than stock. Right: Though we only show Steve at work, Roy Schmidt handled an equal amount in the creation of Boyd Air. Here, Steve can be seen adding those eight extra inches to the width of the hood.

tribute to their craftsmanship.

To begin with, the Impala cowl was retained but the windshield was chopped $2^1/_4$ inches and, while the doors might look stock, they are in fact $4^1/_2$ inches longer than originals. The front fenders are $3^1/_2$ inches longer but five inches thinner, however, the rear fenders are thinner and shorter and the wheelwells on all four fenders were enlarged and pushed forward. The center section of the hood is stock but it was widened four inches on either side whereas the decklid uses two inner '57 Chevy frames spliced together to gain the width and then skinned anew. Incidentally, the original '57 gunsights were replaced with machined aluminum bullets.

Of course, the grille was likewise widened the requisite eight inches, as was the front bumper which was also peaked and shaved of its Dagmars. Decorating the grille opening in true custom car fashion is a similarly widened and shaved chromed floating bar. It was decided to use no mesh behind the bar.

Both front and rear lights are stock '57 Chevy, but that side trim is a combination of new-old-stock pieces and hand-formed parts mounted either side of a cleverly formed appliqué generated using a combination of paint and computer-cut chrome vinyl.

The spacious interior, which was also designed by Chip in the flavor of a fifties Chevy, was fabricated in red leather by Gabe Lopez. The

front seats were originally from a '95 Camaro while the rear seat was a complete fabrication. Other interior features include a modified GM tilt column, Boyds Tri-Grip steering wheel and an instrument panel fitted with Boyds Classic Instruments.

The wide, leather-clad transmission tunnel is home to a shortened Gennie shifter and a Pioneer head unit hooked up to a Boyds/Orion sound system.

Needless to say, Boyd Air was completed on schedule and was duly photographed in February 1997 for the cover of the May 1997 issue of *Hot Rod* magazine and headed up the troops on the *Hot Rod* magazine Power Tour.

Below left: Designed by Chip Foose around a pair of Camaro front seats and a fabricated rear, the interior was stitched in repro '57 fabric and leather by Gabe Lopez. Interior features a Gennie shifter and Boyds Tri-Grip wheel.
Bottom left: Equally resplendent trunk houses a full set of Boyds/Orion amps hooked up to a Pioneer head unit.
Below right: A '96 Corvette LT1 motor is coupled to a 4L60-E transmission and an '85 Corvette third-member with Posi.
Bottom right: It might look stock, but simplicity belies the amount of work that went into the front end. The traditional floating grille bar was widened and shaved to fit.

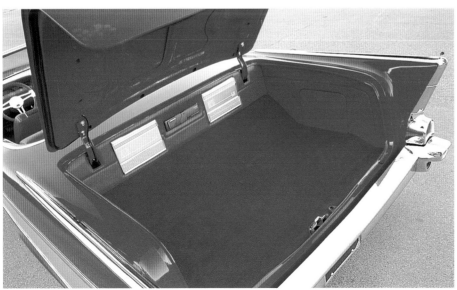

Wes Rydell
'50 CHEVY - GENUINE

Custom four-doors are a rare commodity, particularly in Boydville. Custom four-doors modified to the extent of Wes Rydell's '50 Chevy Fleetline are rarer still. Wes, who hails from Grand Forks, North Dakota, brought the project to Hot Rods by Boyd and worked closely with Chip Foose, who says, "The experience was a lot of fun," to develop this stunningly subtle sedan.

Wes is a tall dude and his the first order of the day was a four-inch stretch in the wheelbase to accommodate his tall frame. Larry Sergejeff subsequently fabricated a ladder-type frame, installing along the way a Chevy S-10 pickup front end and a Chevy Monte Carlo coil-sprung rear, both of which had been supplied by Wes along with a brand new Corvette LT1 motor and transmission.

Once the chassis was up and rolling, assembly of the body began. The modifications are actually extremely extensive, however, the workmanship is such that to an untrained eye, the car could be mistaken for stock—it's far from stock.

To begin with, the roof was cut completely out of the car so that the front windshield posts could be laid back four inches at the top. The windshield was also modified to take the one-piece glass from a '50 Olds—a trick customisers employed in the fifties. At this point the front doors were extended four inches and were shaved of their handles. All four doors are now electrically operated and can be opened from the driver's seats. While the window height remains stock, the B-pillars were leaned back and reshaped for a sleeker, more aerodynamic look.

With the windshield and doors reshaped, work moved to the rear of the car where the decklid was sectioned two inches at the front tapering to zero at the rear. It was then reskinned to flow into the body. Once the decklid modifications were complete, it was possible to drop the rear window and the roof into position. The backlight remains essentially stock, however, the roof was sectioned two inches to remove the crown. While they were at it, Boyd's metal men removed the drip rail to give

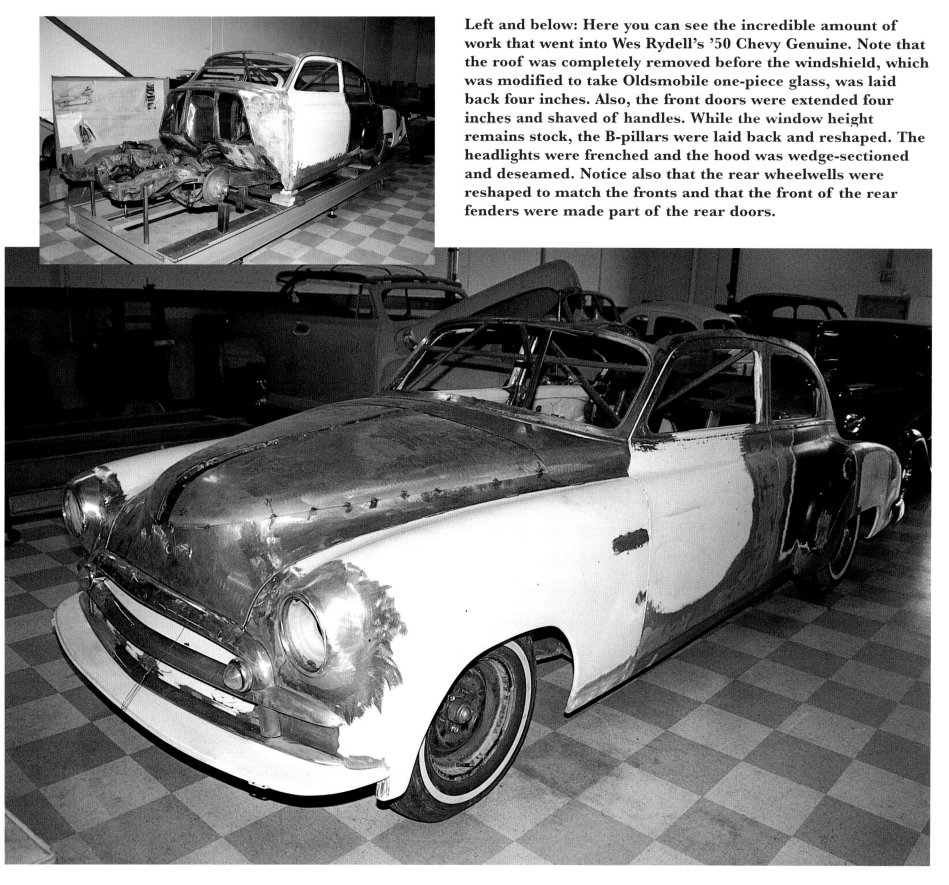

Left and below: Here you can see the incredible amount of work that went into Wes Rydell's '50 Chevy Genuine. Note that the roof was completely removed before the windshield, which was modified to take Oldsmobile one-piece glass, was laid back four inches. Also, the front doors were extended four inches and shaved of handles. While the window height remains stock, the B-pillars were laid back and reshaped. The headlights were frenched and the hood was wedge-sectioned and deseamed. Notice also that the rear wheelwells were reshaped to match the fronts and that the front of the rear fenders were made part of the rear doors.

the roof a smoother, more modern profile.

While the Chevy was being reroofed, the front fenders had the headlights frenched and the hood came in for some serious reworking. Made originally in two halves, the hood was given a taper section starting with $1^3/_4$ inches in front and diminishing to zero at the cowl. The stock seam and resultant trim was also removed.

Though extensive, the body modifications weren't through yet. The leading edge of the rear fenders was added to the back of the rear doors so that the front half of the rear fender is now part of the door. It makes for a very different look especially as the rear wheel opening was also opened up to complement the fronts.

Below left: Here, Robin Hermansen modifies the windshield surround to accept the Oldsmobile one-piece glass.
Below right: Chip Foose completely redesigned the '51 Chevy dash and can be seen here marking out the filled area for the cluster of Classic Instruments.
Bottom right: When it's time to make it happen, as it was when this photograph was taken in February 1997, just a few months before Genuine's introduction, the whole team at Hot Rods by Boyd gets on the job. From left to right that's Karl Jonasson, Conny Jansson and Peter Morrell laying on the floor and Andy Wallin working on the oil cooler.

With external alterations out of the way, work moved inside where a reworked '51 Chevy dash was installed. Smoothed over, the dash was fitted with a new instrument cluster, designed by Chip to accommodate Classic Instruments, billet aluminum air conditioning vents and a glove box. The steering column is a tilt and tele item from a Cadillac chosen because it has column shift but no ugly ignition key. Instead, the key is hidden up under the dash as they are in most hot rods by Boyd. The steering wheel is from a '54 Chevy.

The upholstery was handled by Gabe Lopez, who covered front seats from a Lexus and a hand-formed rear seat in a combination of two different tones as well as perforated gray leather.

Also one-off are the fluted 16 x 7 and 17 x 9.5 wheels which are decorated with Chevrolet center caps and shod with 205/55-16 and 255/50-17 BFGoodrich tires.

Greg Morrell laid down a double-deep coat of DuPont "Double Boyd Black" which is effectively accented with a chrome grille, chrome side trim and chrome window moldings.

Above: Gunmetal gray Corvette LT1 is the powerplant of choice for Wes Rydell's Genuine '50 Chevy.
Left: A great many subtle modifications become invisible in the quality of the workmanship. For example, the whole car was lengthened four inches, the top of the windshield was laid back four inches, the top was sectioned two inches and the decklid was wedge-sectioned two inches tapering to zero. Also notice the frenched taillights and the way that the front portion of the rear fenders have been attached to the rear doors. (Photos courtesy of Rob Fortier and *Street Rodder*.)

WORKS IN PROGRESS

There are plenty of shops around the world that build hot rods and there are a few that build exceptional rods. But Hot Rods by Boyd is unequalled when in comes to comparing the volumes of cars built, some 200 to date, the diversity of the portfolio, everything from a '32 Austin Bantam parade car for Mickey Mouse and Disneyland to Buz Di Vosta's Sportstar, the quality of those cars, quantified by an unprecedented six Oakland Roadster Show winners and the continuing effort to redefine the genre.

Like the man whose name is on the shingle, Hot Rods by Boyd never stands still and never rests on its laurels. Both continually push the boundaries. Boyd has been largely responsible for taking the hot rod out of the backyard and putting it on Wall Street, garnering the cover of *Smithsonian* and myriad other newspapers and periodicals along the way. And, when you're in the business of building hot rods, that is exactly the type of exposure you need to grow your company.

The story of Boyd Coddington and Hot Rods by Boyd is the American Dream personified—small town boy goes to California and makes good. But it doesn't stop there. Over the year and a half this book was in preparation, Hot Rods by Boyd produced rolling sculptures like Picasso with a hot palette: The Boydster, Simply Red, Sportstar, Boydster II, Boyd Air and Genuine, to name but a few. And the hits keep coming. Under construction at the time of going to press were Michael Anthony's '40 convertible, two cars for Fred Warren, a '40 coupe for Butch Martino, an LT5-powered Deuce Roadster for Dan Kruse, a '36 three-window for Dave Sydorick, another '40 convertible for Robbie Madulo and a '48 Ford convertible for Roger Ritzow. We couldn't include them all but on the following pages are some of those cars under construction. Of course, what this means in big picture terms is that in another couple of years, Hot Rods by Boyd will need yet another book to chronicle all the cars built in the ensuing years and there is no doubt that the contents thereof will be of an equal, if not higher, standard.

Left: John Thawley photographed this model of Chip's presentation in his final year at Art Center College of Design. It has been an inspiration to many, not least of which is Fred Warren, who is having Hot Rods by Boyd build him a front-engined roadster version (above). Here, in the early stages, Marcel's is skinning the wooden buck in steel. Meanwhile, Chip, when time allows, is assembling the coupe version with a mid-mounted Chrysler Hemi for power.

Above and left: Just as this book was about to go to print, Michael Anthony's '40 Ford convertible was entering the final stages of construction. Ralph Kirby (above) handled most of the metalwork which included wedge-sectioning the hood $1^3/4$ inches at the front, laying back the windshield $4^1/2$ inches which brought the top down $2^1/2$ inches, frenching the headlights, shaving the handles, a reworked dash, a sunken license plate and custom frenched taillights. Also, all four fender wells were rearched and welded to full-length running boards which parallel the door.

Above: Robin Hermansen applies the hammer to the cowl of Fred Warren's '33 three-window. Begun as a nineties version of The Vern Luce Coupe, the car has now taken on its own identity with hi-tech powertrain, in-board pushrod-operated shocks and numerous body modifications, including filled top, shaved handles and bobbed rear.

Right: Here, in $^1/_5$-scale, is the preliminary clay model for the "Silver Billet," Boyd's tribute to the "Silver Bullet" which did so much to launch his career. Though still in the development stage, Larry Sergejeff has begun assembling a billet aluminum chassis to be powered by an all-aluminum '97 Corvette LS1 engine.

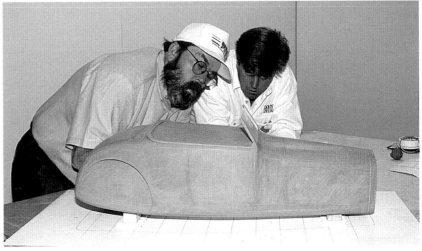

Big Yellow, operated by Bob and Ruth Schoonhoven, is on the road most of the year taking Boyds Wheels and Hot Rods by Boyd to events all across the nation. In this line up, photographed by Scott Williamson, from left to right it is Sportstar, Boydster II, the *Hot Rod* Magazine Giveaway Roadster and Ron Craft's Simply Red.

INDEX